D0031133

Back to Basics: Retirement Planning

by Eric Tyson and Bob Carlson

WILEY

Publisher's Acknowledgments

Editorial Project Manager:
Victoria M. Adang

Senior Acquisitions Editor:
Tracy Boggier

Production Editor:
Siddique Shaik

Cover Images:
(yacht) © WINS86 / Getty Images,
(plane) © WINS86 / Getty Images

Cover Design: Wiley

Back to Basics: Retirement Planning

Published by John Wiley & Sons, Inc.
111 River St.
Hoboken, NJ 07030-5774
http://www.wiley.com

For general information on our other products and services, please contact our Business Development Department in the U.S. at 317-572-3205.

ISBN 978-1-119-47288-9 (pbk); ISBN 978-1-119-47291-9 (ePub); ISBN 978-1-119-47290-2 (ePDF)

Manufactured in the United States of America

10 9 8 7 6 5 4 3 2 1

Contents

1

Planning for Your Future

The ideal time to begin planning for retirement is as soon as you start working. However, for many of you reading this book, this advice comes too late, given the fact you've been in the workforce for a few decades. Don't worry, though. It's never too late to start planning. Studies of retirees show those who are most content in retirement are those who did some amount of planning, even if it was a small amount. Planning is how you match your resources with your goals and expectations and identify where adjustments need to be made.

This chapter discusses important themes that run throughout the book: the value of planning ahead and getting on the best path as soon as possible, the importance of taking personal responsibility, and the significance of taking a long-term perspective to make the most of your senior years. We also discuss how to keep the right focus to optimize your retirement planning.

Planning for the Longer Term

Planning doesn't sound fun, and for many people, it isn't one of life's most enjoyable activities. But nearly everyone values the benefits of proper planning: peace of mind, financial security, more options and choices, improved health, and a better lifestyle.

During your senior years, you have many choices about different financial issues. You can change some of the decisions after you make them, but others can't be changed. If you decide to make changes, you have fewer years to benefit from the new choices. That's why as you approach your senior years, planning your finances is more important than it was earlier in life.

In the following sections, we discuss the important issues that warrant your planning attention, explain why you should take responsibility for making that happen (even if you hire some help), and quantify the value of your taking our advice.

Identifying long-term planning issues

What's on your mind (or should be on your mind) regarding your financial future? Consider how many of the issues in the following sections require long-term planning.

Leaving an employer and deciding what to do with your retirement account money

When you change jobs, get laid off, or retire, you often are faced with choices about when and how to withdraw money from retirement accounts — such as 401(k)s or 403(b)s — and minimizing the tax hit from doing so. Moving money is a decision you have to make today, but don't make light of this decision because the decision affects how much money you'll have in the decades to come.

Some employer plans allow you to keep retirement money in place even if you're no longer employed with the company. You may choose to accept the offer to keep money in place if the plan has good investment options and low costs. Planning retirement account withdrawals requires long-term tax planning if you want to make the withdrawals in the best way possible. For more information on handling retirement accounts, see Chapter 5.

_____

_____

_____

Determining whether you can afford to retire and how much you can safely spend per year

To assess whether you can afford to retire and how much you'll be able to spend after you do retire, you have to do some analysis relating to your spending habits and investing holdings and temperament. And, to be sure that you don't run out of money, you also need to consider a wide range of scenarios for how your investments may perform in the years ahead.

As with other aspects in life, differentiate between the things you can control and the things you can't. The economy will go through recessions and the stock market will decline. Predicting their timing, depth, and duration is beyond anyone's control. Although you can't control these events, you can be prepared for them. Your plan should reflect that by having some flexibility and, if possible, a cushion.

Deciding when to begin collecting Social Security

Deciding when to begin collecting your Social Security is a complicated decision that's affected by many factors, including tax laws, your earnings and your spouse's earnings, and marital status, among others. As we discuss in Chapter 8, you have to look years ahead to make an appropriate decision.

_____

_____

_____

Weighing the option to buy more life insurance

When others are dependent on your employment income, you may need some life insurance coverage. And, depending on your specific assets, the type of life insurance you may most benefit from may change over the years.

To determine your life insurance needs, you should have a good sense of your current financial assets and current and future obligations.

Developing your estate plan

Your financial circumstances will change in the years ahead, and so too will tax and probate laws. Planning your estate involves many issues, including ensuring your own financial security, taking care of your affairs in the event you're unable to do so yourself, and protecting and providing for your heirs.

Taking personal responsibility for your financial future

Our lives are filled with responsibilities — jobs, family obligations, bills, household maintenance. We all try to make time for friends, fun, and recreation as well.

With all of these competing demands, it's no wonder that many folks find that planning for their financial future continually gets pushed to the back burner. Most people don't have the time, desire, or expertise to make good financial decisions. But you've taken a huge step to erase those obstacles in buying this book.

From this point forward, we urge you to always remember that you — and only you — can take full responsibility for your financial future. Of course, you can hire advisors or delegate certain issues to a willing and competent spouse or other beloved relative. But, at the end of the day, it's your money on the line. Delegating your responsibilities without knowledge, understanding, and some involvement is a recipe for disaster. You could end up without vital insurance, be taken advantage of in terms of fees, or even defrauded among other unsavory outcomes.

Saving and planning sooner and smarter pays off

The sooner you get control over and optimize your finances, the bigger your payoff will be.

_____

_____

_____

You should never rush into making changes that you don't understand and haven't had time to properly research. Procrastination comes with many costs, including lost financial opportunities. Creating a financial plan and sticking to it is important when planning for retirement. Chapter 3 helps you make your own plan.

Keys to Retirement Planning

Although you may like to consider other factors — such as your health, relationships with friends and family, and interests and activities — as more important than money, the bottom line is that money and personal financial health are extra-important factors to your retirement lifestyle.

Getting caught up in planning the financial part of your future is easy. After all, money is measurable and so much revolves around the money component of retirement planning. So what can you do to successfully plan for retirement? You could simply work really hard and spend lots of time making as much money as possible. But what would be the point if you have little free time to enjoy yourself and others?

Fortunately you can implement the following strategies when planning for retirement.

Saving drives wealth

You may think a high income is key to having a prosperous retirement, but research shows that the best way to retirement bliss is to save. Research demonstrates that wealth accumulation is driven more by the choice to save (rather than spend) than it is by a person's income.

 It's not what you make but what you keep (save) that's important to building wealth. Of course, earning more should make it easier to save, but most folks allow their spending to increase with their incomes.

Keeping your balance

Most people we know have more than one goal when it comes to their money and personal situations. People want to save for retirement, pay for their children's college education, travel, pursue expensive hobbies, and have money available for any number of things. Having multiple goals competing for limited dollars is often the norm. Thus, you must decide how to trade off competing goals, which requires personal considerations and balance in one's life.

Unless you have really deep pockets and modest goals, you need to prioritize and value each of your goals.

Planning is a process

To have a good retirement you almost always need to be planning. Financial planning is a process. Too many people develop financial plans and then think they're finished.

A plan is based on assumptions and forecasts. However, no plan — no matter how carefully it's developed — gets all the assumptions and forecasts correct. Even your best guesses may miss the mark. So every few years, you need to review your plan.

As you're reviewing, assess how much reality differed from your assumptions. Sometimes you'll be pleasantly surprised. Your portfolio may earn more than you expected, or you may spend less than you estimated.

Other times the review won't be as pleasant. The markets may have dragged down your portfolio returns. Or your spending may have exceeded your estimates. In either case, you aren't reaching your goals.

_____

_____

_____

Even if you do meet the mark in most instances, you are still never really done planning and revising. You're bound to experience changes in your life, the economy, the markets, tax law, and other areas. You may come across new opportunities that weren't available a few years ago or that weren't right for you then but make sense now. You need to continually adapt your plan to these changes. You may need to adjust your spending or change your investment portfolio.

You don't have to be obsessive. Daily, or even quarterly, changes in your portfolio that are different from the plan aren't a reason to go back to the drawing board. But every year or so (or when you have a major change in your personal situation), take a fresh look. Review the plan and your progress. Figure out what went right and what went wrong. Decide whether your goals or situation have changed and whether any adjustments are needed. Finally, implement the new plan and enjoy life. After all, that's what the money is for.

Retirement Worries

What are the worries and fears of retirees and senior citizens? Thanks to research and studies, we know what people are concerned about, and we discuss everything you need to know in this section. Knowing this information helps you plan ahead and prepare. The challenge for most people is this: Retirement is financially unlike any other period in their lives because retirees generally are

- **Working less (or not at all):** Retirees have more free time in which to spend money but have less earned income.

- **Living off investments and monthly benefit checks:** During most wage earners' working years, their income exceeds their spending, and psychologically they get used to that. For many retirees, on the other hand, spending exceeds income.

- **Using more medical services:** Retirees use more medical services even if they have comparably good health within their peer group. They need more medical tests, spend more on prescription and over-the-counter drugs, and have more medical problems.

Many seniors and near-seniors understand these changes, which is why they worry about money and other retirement issues. Many fears revolve around concerns about running out

_____

_____

_____

of money. In the following sections, we discuss these specific anxieties, why they exist, and what you can do to address them.

Running out of money

In Eric's prior work with near-retirees and retirees, one worry far exceeded all others among his clients: the fear of running out of money. Even people who possessed what seemed like plenty of money worried about having enough. Later in this section, we enumerate the sources of this fear and give you our take on what you can do about it.

Some seniors deal with the problem of running out of money by continuing to work during retirement. You may need to make some slight adjustments and work part time during retirement or even start a small business to help make ends meet.

Supporting others

Plenty of seniors are concerned about making ends meet for the duration of their retirement. But seniors aren't egocentrically focused on their own finances. In fact, to the contrary. They're also concerned about other family members whom they're taking care of financially. More than four in ten (44 percent) retired Americans support one or more people living outside their home. Among those receiving support are

- Adult children (53 percent)
- Grandchildren (37 percent)
- Elderly parents (12 percent)

Before hitting retirement, plenty of near-seniors get "sandwiched" providing for their own children and helping their aging parents. How can near-seniors who then end up retiring accomplish all of this? Consider the following reasons:

- **They continue to be frugal.** People who saved and invested during their working years generally continue their frugality in retirement. The best savers often have trouble learning to live off their money in retirement.

- **They have a desire to help loved ones.** Most seniors adore their offspring, and nothing makes most seniors happier than helping their children, grandchildren, and extended families. Sometimes you also have to help your aging parents.

- **They have fears about outliving their available funds and becoming a burden to others.** There's great uncertainty about how long any one person or couple will live as well as what will happen to their personal health. So most people assume that they'll live longer and perhaps need extensive medical care later in life; as a result, they keep more money saved. However, retirees often overlook the fact that Social Security keeps paying benefits as long as you live. Money left invested also will continue compounding and growing over the long term — so long as it's invested intelligently (see Chapter 7 for details).

- **They spend less on many things later in retirement.** Qualitatively, as soon as folks cut back on work, they spend a lot less on work-related expenses — from clothing to commuting to buying fewer services — compared with when they had far greater demands on their time. Even among active seniors, as mobility is reduced later in retirement, travel and shopping also are reduced. Yes, people may spend more on some things (like health care) as they age, but in general, they spend less, which leads to folks having more of their money last longer than they may have guessed.

- **They live in a wealthy country with an economic bounty.** America is still a wealthy nation and provides a relatively high standard of living for the vast majority of people. Yes, in the years and decades ahead, the United States will likely be sharing its economic superpower status with some other emerging, higher-growth economies, but its economy should continue to grow.

Addressing your worries

Dr. Frank Luntz, author of *What Americans Really Want . . . Really* (Hyperion), is a prolific pollster and focus group organizer who has studied retirees through focus groups and research surveys. He developed a list of "The Seven Most Frequently Asked Questions About Retirement" by people age 60 and older. As we introduce the questions, we include explanations on how to address your worries and feel better about each of them.

The first six items deal with a senior's ability to manage his cash flow and match up his income to his expenses. The last item on the list — concerning maintaining independence and mobility — is partly related to income and expenses, too. Here are Dr. Luntz's questions, along with our explanations:

- **Will I be able to afford health care when I get too old to work? Am I one medical emergency away from bankruptcy and ruin?** Yes, you should be able to afford health care in retirement, and, no, a medical emergency or major illness doesn't have to bankrupt you. Medicare is a pretty comprehensive major medical insurance plan that can include prescription drug coverage. You also can buy long-term care insurance and a Medicare supplement.

- **Is Social Security going to be there for me?** Yes, it should be. We discuss this worry at length in Chapter 8, and show you why you shouldn't be worried about it.

- **Will prescription drugs be so expensive that I'll be forced to choose between medications and food?** No. The vast majority of prescription drugs have been in the market for many years and have competition from generics, which keeps costs down. You also can purchase prescription drug coverage through Medicare.

- **Will I run out of money before I run out of years?** No. Social Security benefits, which increase annually with inflation, continue for your life. To ensure that your invested dollars stretch for as long as possible, be sure to follow our investing advice in Chapters 5 and 7. Finally, if you're a homeowner, equity in your home provides another financial safety net in case you need additional resources later in your retirement.

- **Will I be a financial and physical burden on my spouse or my children? Will I lose my independence and mobility?** These last two questions are the hardest to answer and address. Financially, you should be fine in the long term with the advice provided in this book. However, you can't predict your health. As you age later in your elderly years, you'll experience an inevitable reduction in mobility and ability to do some things you've historically been able to do. You can make the most of your health for as many years as possible by taking sensible steps to maintain your good health.

_____

_____

_____

2

Develop a Retirement Plan

Although many folks dream about retiring, few are preparing. A survey conducted by the Employee Benefit Research Institute regarding Americans' planning for retirement found that:

- Only about 65 percent of working adults surveyed are saving for retirement.
- Of those who are saving, 65 percent have a nest egg of less than $50,000.
- About half of survey participants simply guess at the amount of their retirement needs.

Your future plans are important enough to deserve more than a guess. But we understand that your free time is valuable and that you have more interesting things to do than analyze numbers to determine your retirement needs. So in this chapter, we provide retirement planning insights and tips without taking too much of your time. Before we dig into the financial part of planning retirement, though, we discuss some general retirement topics that are just as important. You need to have a firm grasp of these items as well.

When to Retire

Retiring sounds appealing when you've had a frustrating stretch at a job you don't particularly enjoy. But some folks enjoy working and aren't eager to have wide-open daily schedules day after day, week after week. Deciding when to retire and what to do in retirement is an intensely personal decision. There are many financial and personal considerations and questions, and we address them in this chapter.

Even when you're healthy, the job market may not be. Your employer could suffer financial hardship and reduce its workforce. Or maybe you'll be lucky enough to retire early (even though it's unplanned) because your employer offers you a buyout package that's too good to turn down. Or worse, you may lose your job with little notice and few benefits.

Ideally, when caught in one of these situations, you would obtain another job and continue it until your planned retirement age. Unfortunately, events may not unfold that way. The economy, the job market, and your age could work against you. Finding another job, at a compensation level you're willing to work for, may not be possible.

Even when you leave a full-time career voluntarily, you may plan to work part time for a few years. Or you may assume that if the first years of retirement are more expensive than planned, you could return to work at least part time. Yet, a part-time job you assumed would be easy to find may not be available at all or may be available at a much lower level of pay than you expected.

How Much You Really Need for Retirement

Most people have a long-term financial goal of retiring someday. For some, doing so means leaving work entirely. To others, simply cutting back on work or doing something completely different on a part-time basis is most appealing.

_____

_____

_____

If you don't plan to work well into your golden years, you need a reasonable chunk of money in order to maintain a particular lifestyle in the absence of your normal employment income. The following sections help you determine how much money you need and come to grips with those numbers.

What portion of income you need

If you're like most people, you need less money to live on in retirement than during your working years. That's because in retirement most people don't need to save any of their income and many of their work-related expenses (commuting, work clothes, and such) go away or greatly decrease. With less income, most retirees find they pay less in taxes too.

On the flip side, some categories of expenses may go up in retirement. With more free time on your hands, you may spend more on entertainment, meals out, and travel. The costs for prescription drugs and other medical expenses can also add up.

So what portion of your income do you need as you make your retirement plan? The answer isn't simple. Everyone's situation is unique, so examine your current expenditures and consider how they may change in the years ahead. Check out

Chapters 3 and 4 for more information on budgeting and managing your expenses in retirement.

To figure out how much money you need, keep the following statistics in mind. Studies have shown that retirees typically spend 65 to 80 percent of their pre-retirement income during their retirement years. People at the lower end of this range typically

- Save a large portion of their annual earnings during their working years
- Don't have a mortgage or any other debt in retirement
- Are higher-income earners who don't anticipate leading a lifestyle in retirement that's reflective of their current high-income lifestyle

Those who spend at the higher end of the range tend to have the following characteristics:

- Save little or none of their annual earnings before retirement
- Still have a significant mortgage or growing rent to pay in retirement

_____

_____

_____

- Need nearly all current income to meet their current lifestyle
- Have expensive hobbies that they have more time to pursue

We can't offer a definitive answer as to how much you need to have for your retirement. Just make sure you carefully look at all your expenses and figure out how they may change (see Chapter 3).

What the numbers mean

When determining how much money you need for your retirement plans, you want to think in terms of your goals and how much you need to save per month to reach your desired goal given your current situation.

In Eric's previous work as a personal financial planner and lecturer, he met people who had done some basic number crunching or had consulted a financial advisor. Far too often, these folks got a number — a big number like $3.8 million — stuck in their heads. That number was the size of the nest egg they needed to achieve a particular standard of living throughout their retirement.

_____

_____

_____

Rather than obsessing about a large number, examine your own standard of living that can be provided by the assets you've accumulated or will likely accumulate by a preferred retirement age. You can then begin to put the numbers into perspective for your own individual case (see the "Calculate the Numbers" section later in this chapter).

The Components of Your Retirement Plan

To meet your retirement needs, you need a firm grasp of what resources are available to help you. In addition to government benefits such as Social Security, employer retirement accounts and personal investments round out most people's retirement income sources. This section takes a closer look at these elements.

Social Security retirement benefits

Social Security is intended to provide a subsistence level of income in retirement for basic living necessities such as food, shelter, and clothing. However, Social Security wasn't designed to be a retiree's sole source of income. When planning for retirement, you'll likely need to supplement your expected Social Security benefits with personal savings, investments, and employer retirement accounts. (Refer to Chapter 8 for more discussion on Social Security.)

If you're still working, you can estimate your Social Security retirement benefits by looking at your most recent Social Security benefits statement, which the federal government makes available online each year to adults age 25 and older. You can access your latest statement online at www.ssa.gov (click on the My Social Security tab on the home page) or by calling 800-772-1213 and requesting form SSA-7004 ("Request for Social Security Statement").

Like many people, you may be concerned about your Social Security. You may be afraid it won't be there when you retire. Although you may have to wait until you're slightly older to collect benefits or endure more of your benefits being taxed, rest assured. Congress has been reluctant over the years to make major negative changes to Social Security because doing so would risk upsetting a large and highly active voting bloc of retirees.

With your Social Security benefits statement in hand, you can see how much Social Security you've already earned and review how the Social Security Administration (SSA) determines these numbers. With this information, you can better plan for your retirement and make important retirement planning decisions.

Your estimated benefits statement

Your Social Security benefits statement can give you important information about your estimated retirement benefits. On Page 2 of this annual statement, you see information like the following (unless you don't have enough *work credits*, which are awarded for every year you earn money):

You have earned enough credits to qualify for benefits. At your current earnings rate, if you continue working until:

Your full retirement age (67 years), your payment would be about $1,543 a month

Age 70, your payment would be about $1,924 a month

If you stop working and start receiving benefits at age 62, your payment would be about $1,064 a month

These statements are self-explanatory. (We explain in Chapter 8 how the credit-earning part of Social Security works.)

How your benefits are estimated

Along with your benefits estimates, the SSA also discloses the assumptions used to come up with your numbers and some important caveats. You should understand the assumptions behind the estimates we talk about in the preceding section. Why? These are projections, and depending on your earnings in the years ahead, your expected benefits may change. Here's what the SSA says:

> Generally, the older you are and the closer you are to retirement, the more accurate the retirement estimates will be because they are based on a longer work history with fewer uncertainties such as earnings fluctuations and future law changes.

If you stop and consider this assumption, it makes sense and is true of almost any forecast or estimate. The further into the future you try to project something, the more likely it is that the estimates may be off base.

To understand what could throw off future estimates, keep the following in mind as you dig deeper into the SSA's assumptions:

_____

_____

_____

If you have enough work credits, we estimated your benefit amounts using your average earnings over your working lifetime. For 2017 and later (up to retirement age), we assumed you'll continue to work and make about the same as you did in 2015 or 2016. We can't provide your actual benefit amount until you apply for benefits. And that amount may differ from the estimates stated above because:

(1) Your earnings may increase or decrease in the future.

(2) After you start receiving benefits, they will be adjusted for cost-of-living increases.

(3) Your estimated benefits are based on current law. The law governing benefit amounts may change.

In other words, the SSA assumes that your future earnings will annually be about the same as your earnings in the most recent couple of years. Therefore, as their own cautions highlight, if you expect your future work earnings to change from your most recent years' employment earnings, your expected Social Security retirement benefits also will change.

Don't get hung up over expected cost-of-living increases. When we walk you through the retirement number crunching later in this chapter, these increases are incorporated into the analysis.

If you want to delve into different scenarios for your Social Security benefits, use the SSA's online Retirement Estimator at www.socialsecurity. gov/estimator.

Investments

The many types of investments you may have are an important component of your retirement plan. These investments may come in various forms, such as bank accounts, brokerage accounts, mutual fund accounts, and so on. Your investments may or may not be in retirement accounts. Even if they aren't, they still can be earmarked to help with your retirement.

Take an inventory of your savings and investments by gathering recent copies of your statements from the following types of accounts or investment options:

- Bank accounts — checking (especially if it holds excess savings), savings, certificates of deposit, and so on

- IRA accounts

- Taxable accounts at brokers and mutual funds

- Employer retirement accounts, including
  - Profit-sharing plans
  - Employee stock ownership plans (ESOPs)
  - 401(k)s, 403(b)s, and so forth
- Investment real estate

We provide information in Chapters 4 through 7 about retirement investments. At this point, you simply need to take an inventory of your current assets and use that information in the "Calculate the Numbers" section later in this chapter to determine where you stand regarding retirement planning.

Your home's equity

If you've owned a home over the years, and it has a decent amount of *equity* (the difference between its market value and the mortgage debt owed on it) in it, you can tap into that equity to provide for your retirement. To tap into your home's equity, you have two primary options:

- **You can sell your home.** After you sell your home, you can either buy a less costly one or rent.

_____
_____
_____

- **You can take out a reverse mortgage.** With a *reverse mortgage*, you draw income against your home, which is accumulated as a debt balance to be paid once the home is sold.

If you'd like to tap your home's equity to help with retirement, consider how much equity you would use.

Talk Over Your Plan

When beginning your retirement planning, make sure you sit down with your spouse and coordinate each person's plan together. Doing so may seem obvious, but it's an important step. Discussions about retirement plans need to begin long before retirement. Even when one spouse is doing most of the financial planning for retirement, both spouses need to agree on the nonfinancial aspects of their senior years. And the spouse who is not doing as much of the financial planning needs to know the overall financial situation.

Couples should begin discussing the following topics at least five years before retirement.

- Should each of you retire? If so, when would each prefer to begin retirement?

- Would retirement be complete, or is part-time work a possibility for either spouse?

- Where will you live during retirement?

- How will each of you spend nonworking time during retirement? What things will you do together and which will you do separately?

- Have you estimated how much money you will need to support your retirement plans? If so, how much will you need and how close are you to having it?

- What is the plan for spending your retirement funds, and what is the plan for investing the funds?

- What assets and accounts do you own, where are they, and how are they invested?

- What legacy do you hope to leave? Is there a plan for fulfilling that goal?

- What is your estate plan and where are the documents?

- What role will children and parents play in the rest of your lives? Will you move to live near either adult children or aging parents? Do you plan to help or support either of them if needed? If this is a second marriage for either spouse, what are the plans for any children of the prior marriage?

• What is the attitude of each of you to aging, and how do you expect to react to it?

Calculate the Numbers

For purposes of retirement planning, what matters most is where you stand today as far as reaching your goal. So you need to crunch some numbers to get a handle on your situation. One of the best ways to do so is to use available retirement calculators, either online or with a hard copy workbook. These resources can walk you through the calculations needed to figure how much you should be saving to reach your retirement goal. The information you collect and the questions you answer earlier in this chapter allow you to begin crunching the numbers.

Among the mass-market website tools, we like the one from T. Rowe Price. Visit www.troweprice.com and search for "retirement calculator." The T. Rowe Price web-based Retirement Income Calculator is a user-friendly tool, and the website says it takes about 10 minutes to complete. If you're organized and have your documents handy, you may cruise through it that quickly, but otherwise you'll more than likely need 20 to 30 minutes.

In the following sections, we walk you through steps for using the T. Rowe Price retirement planning tools to get a better assessment of your financial numbers as you prepare for retirement. We use T. Rowe Price as an example, but please note that you can select another company's tool if you prefer.

Assumptions and how they work

When estimating the amount of money you will need in retirement, make sure you're aware of the different assumptions used. This section details those assumptions.

In this section, we specifically look at the T. Rowe Price assumptions and online calculator. In order for you to make the best use of this site, we review the following important key assumptions. If you choose not to use this online tool, you can use the discussion of the assumptions that follow for other retirement planning tools.

- **Asset allocation:** The calculator asks you to enter your current allocation (mix of major investment classes) and then to select an allocation for after you're retired. For the retirement allocation, you can choose a fixed 40 percent stock, 40 percent bond, 20 percent money fund, or you can have the mix gradually shift away from stocks each year that you're in retirement. Either choice is fine, but we have a slight preference for the latter of the two options.

  The calculator doesn't include real estate as a possible asset. If you own real estate as an investment you should treat those assets as a stock-like investment, because they have similar long-term risk and return characteristics. You should calculate your equity in investment real estate.

- **Age of retirement:** For this assumption, you plug in your preferred age of retirement. Depending on how the analysis works out, you can always go back and plug in a different age. Sometimes folks are pleasantly surprised that their combined accumulated resources provide them with a decent enough standard of living that they can consider retiring sooner than they thought.

- **Social Security:** The T. Rowe Price calculator asks whether you want to include expected Social Security benefits. We'd rather that the calculator didn't pose this question because you definitely should include your Social Security benefits in the calculations. Don't buy into the speculation that the program will disappear and leave you with little to nothing. For the vast majority of people, Social Security benefits are an important component of their retirement income, so make sure to include them.

  Based on your current income, the T. Rowe Price retirement program will automatically plug in your estimated Social Security benefits. So long as your income hasn't changed or won't change dramatically, using their estimated number should be fine. Alternatively, you could input your own number using a recent Social Security benefits statement if you have one handy. Or use the Retirement Estimator at the Social Security website (www.socialsecurity.gov/estimator).

After you enter your personal information and decide on the preceding assumptions, you're ready to finish the calculations. The T. Rowe Price calculator assumes that you want to replace 70 percent of your pre-retirement income through age 95. So Price's completed analysis shows how much you can live on per month and then compares that with what you're projected to need to maintain 70 percent of your current income. The calculations include doing 1,000 market simulations, and it works 70 percent of the time.

Making the numbers work

After you crunch the numbers, you may discover you need to save at a rate that isn't doable. Don't despair. You have the following options to lessen the depressingly high savings you may need:

- **Boost your investment returns.** Reduce your taxes while investing: While you're still working, be sure to take advantage of retirement savings accounts, especially when you can gain free matching money from your employer or you're eligible for the special tax credit from the government. When investing money outside of retirement accounts, take care to minimize taxes. For more on investing strategies, see Chapter 7.

- **Work (a little) more.** Extend the number of years you're willing to work, or consider working part time for a few years past the age you were expecting to stop working.

- **Reduce your spending.** The more you spend today, the more years you'll have to work to meet your savings goal. See Chapter 3 to find out how to manage your spending in retirement.

- **Use your home's equity.** If you didn't factor using some of your home's equity into your retirement nest egg, consider doing so. Some people are willing to trade down to a less costly property in retirement. You also can take a reverse mortgage to tap some of your property's equity. We talk more about home equity and reverse mortgages in the earlier section "Your home's equity."

Dealing with excess money

When Eric was working as a financial counselor, one of his favorite parts of the job was going over the retirement analysis with clients who had accumulated more than they needed to achieve their desired lifestyle. Often, this was a surprise to the client, so some people had a hard time believing the good news.

If you find yourself with extra money, the good news is at least you don't have to worry about making sure you can continue your current standard of living during retirement. In this situation, consider taking either of the following actions:

- **Enhance your retirement.** We're not suggesting that the only way to a happy retirement is to spend money, but don't be afraid to enjoy yourself. While you're still healthy, travel, eat out, take some classes, and do whatever else interests you. Remember that come the end of your life, you can't take your money with you.

- **Earmark a portion of your assets for your beneficiaries.** You may want to leave something for your family members as well as other beneficiaries, such as your place of worship and charities. If so, you need to determine the approximate dollar amount for each of the beneficiaries.

Spending Your Nest Egg

A day will come when you have to consider how much of your retirement nest egg you can spend each year. For some retirees, that day happens when they retire; for others it occurs years into retirement. And for a small minority, they never tap into their nest egg in retirement. The following sections discuss important considerations as you decide when and how to spend your nest egg.

The 4 percent rule

The vast majority of retirees need to live off at least a portion of their investment portfolio's returns. If you're in this majority, a logical concern you may have is determining how much of your portfolio and its returns you can use each year, while still having some reasonable expectation that your portfolio will last throughout your retirement. That's where the 4 percent rule comes into play.

Analyses and studies have found that if you withdraw about 4 percent of your nest egg in the first year of retirement and then bump that amount up by a few percent per year for increases in the cost of living, your portfolio should last at least 30 years.

Here's an example to illustrate: Suppose you retire with about $500,000 invested in a balanced portfolio of stocks and bonds. The 4 percent rule would suggest that you plan on taking about $20,000 from this retirement nest egg in your first year of retirement. If you assume a 3 percent rate of inflation, in the second year you would take $20,600.

Factors affecting your use of retirement assets

The 4 percent rule is a starting point to consider for typical folks planning retirement and expecting to maintain a balanced portfolio. However, 4 percent may not be the ideal number for you based on the amount of money you have in savings. For example, if you want to ensure that your money lasts even longer, you could try 3 percent withdrawals rather than 4 percent withdrawals.

Here are some important factors affecting whether you should use 4 percent or a slightly different number:

- **Actual expenses relative to your income:** You may find early in your retirement that you don't need 4 percent from your financial assets to make ends meet. This occurs perhaps because you still have some employment income coming in or your monthly checks from Social Security and pensions are sufficient for your spending needs. If that's the case and you can delay tapping into your investment returns or income, then by all means do so.

One challenge of planning ahead is that you can't predict unexpectedly large expenses; you can only make intelligent guesses.

- **Health and life expectancy:** If you come from a family where folks routinely live a long time, you want to ensure that your money lasts as long as you do. You may have to use an investment withdrawal rate of less than 4 percent, such as 3 percent to 3.5 percent.

- **Investment performance:** If you're an investor who's less willing to be reasonably aggressive with asset allocation (say a 50/50 mix between growth investments like stocks and real estate and lending investments like bonds), consider using a retirement withdrawal figure of less than 4 percent. Conversely, if you're willing to be more aggressive, you could use 4.5 percent to 5 percent. However, be aware of the potential downside of the financial markets producing lower-than-expected returns over a number of years.

- **Risk tolerance:** How comfortable are you with taking risk? If you're a nervous wreck about putting even a small portion of your money in something other than bank accounts or Treasury bonds, using 4 percent withdrawals is too high a number.

3

Managing Expenses

By the time most people reach their retirement years, they've been managing money for several decades. That's a good thing. Between the knowledge acquired over time and the valuable lessons learned in the school of life, people enter retirement a lot wiser and more money savvy than they were as young adults.

Making the most of your senior years and your money requires you to plan ahead and be prepared for some surprises. This chapter helps you manage your expenses and spending throughout your retirement to make the transition as easy as possible.

How Spending Changes in Retirement

Seeing how much other retirees spend can help you plan your own retirement better. The federal government collects and collates consumer spending data that can be analyzed many ways. With this information, we examine here how people's spending habits change after age 65, an age by which many people retire or are close to retiring.

The average number of people in the "consumer unit" (household) changes over time. As we were analyzing how spending changed in retirement compared with the years immediately before retirement, we noted the following changes in average household size:

Age	Average Number of People in Household
55–64	2.1
65–74	1.8
75+	1.5

The primary reason for the decline in the average number of people in a household after age 65 and 75 is because of the passing of an elderly spouse. You have to adjust for changes in the number of people in the household to make better sense of some of the numbers. For example, you would expect a smaller number of people to eat less food.

The first column in Table 3-1 shows the average expenditures for households that fall into the 55-to-64-year-old age bracket. Of course, these are national averages and may differ greatly from how much and where you spend your own money. (*Remember:* Taxes weren't accurately captured by this survey and thus are omitted; though we do discuss them briefly later.)

Expenditures	Age 55–64	Age 65–74	Age 75+
Total expenditures	$54,783	–11.8%	–19.0%
Housing	$17,611	–8.3%	–4.3%
Transportation	$9,377	–16.1%	–34.4%
Food	$6,357	–2.0%	–13.3%
At home	$3,711	7.6%	0.6%
Out	$2,646	–15.5%	–32.9%
Health care	$3,825	45.8%	61.5%
Entertainment	$3,036	–7.1%	–37.8%
Cash contributions (to loved ones and charities)	$2,163	9.6%	48.3%
Apparel	$1,622	–0.7%	–34.8%

Table 3-1: *Per Person Changes in Expenditures by Age Group*

Here are the highlights of what's shown in the data from Table 3-1:

- Overall expenses per person decline significantly as do the vast majority of the individual expense categories, which are ranked in order of their overall amounts (at ages 55–64).

- Expenses drop even more later in retirement (age 75+). This decrease makes sense given that many folks downsize their housing and become less mobile. Transportation and entertainment expanses also drop significantly.

- Later in retirement, apparel expenses drop. That's because most older retirees shop less and are more content to wear what they have rather than buying more.

- Spending on food declines due to eating out less. Spending on food consumed at home rises a little.

- Health care spending per person goes up significantly.

- Cash donations went up too, especially at age 75+. As people with excess money approach the end of their lives, they become more interested and motivated to give away money to loved ones and favorite charities.

It's also useful to look at the household level changes in expenditures (refer to Table 3-2) that aren't adjusted for changes in household size because they reflect an average or typical household's changes in expenditures over the retirement years.

Expenditures	Age 55–64	Age 65–74	Age 75+
Total expenditures	$54,783	−24.4%	−42.1%
Housing	$17,611	−21.4%	−31.7%
Transportation	$9,377	−28.1%	−53.2%
Food	$6,357	−16.0%	−38.1%
At home	$3,711	−7.8%	−28.1%
Out	$2,646	−27.5%	−52.1%
Health care	$3,825	24.9%	15.4%
Entertainment	$3,036	−20.4%	−55.6%
Cash Contributions	$2,163	−6.0%	5.9%
Apparel	$1,622	−14.9%	−53.4%

Table 3-2: *Household Changes in Expenditures by Age Group*

Consider these highlights from the data in Table 3-2:

- Large, overall reductions occur in total expenditures and in most of the individual expense categories. These reductions raise an interesting issue for your planning purposes as a couple and consideration of how your individual health and expected longevity affect your household's spending. If both you and your spouse have and expect to maintain excellent health, you should probably use the per person changes in spending from Table 3-1.

- Note the bigger declines in housing expenses. Unlike food costs, for example, which are driven by the number of people in a household, housing costs are more fixed, so these bigger declines would be more typical of what an average retiree experiences. To realize these housing cost reductions though, older retirees downsize their homes or take advantage of property tax breaks available through many towns and cities.

- Although taxes weren't accurately captured in this survey, they clearly would have shown a significant reduction in the retirement years when most people earn far less income and also are paying much less in Social Security and Medicare taxes, which applies only to employment earnings.

Managing Your Expenses

Most people do a decent job managing their expenses in retirement. After all, by the time people reach retirement, they have decades of experience managing their finances and spending. That said, plenty of people make mistakes and worry about things they shouldn't worry about while overlooking issues that they should have paid closer attention to. That's what this section is all about.

Bigger-picture issues

Before we dig into specific expenditures, we want to first discuss some overarching retirement spending issues and concerns. Here are the important points to keep in mind:

- **After you retire and stop earning employment income, one of the cash outflows that should go away is saving more money.** Some folks early in retirement continue to effectively save by not using all the money coming in (for example, from Social Security, pensions, and so on).

They scrimp and save and do without when they don't need to. If your retirement analysis shows that you don't need to save anymore, then don't!

- **Throughout your retirement, you need to consider inflation.** When you examine your spending now or next year, remember that you're examining a snapshot or point in time. Over the years, most (but not all) items increase in price (3 percent per year is a good average to use because that is what consumer price inflation in the United States has averaged over many years). So plan accordingly by considering not just your current spending but also your spending in the years and decades ahead.

- **Remain optimistic about your retirement.** One study from a large accounting firm ominously warned that about 60 percent of middle-class retirees would probably run out of money if they maintained their pre-retirement lifestyles. Technically that may be true, but an important detail the study failed to mention is the vast majority of retirees spend less — in some cases quite a bit less — when they retire in comparison to their pre-retirement spending.

In the sections that follow, we go through important expense categories and discuss what typically happens to retirees regarding those expenses and offer money-saving opportunities.

Taxes

One fringe benefit of ceasing work and getting over the financial impact of losing that income is the associated and often dramatic reduction in income taxes — both federal and state — as well as in FICA (Social Security and Medicare) taxes and possibly local taxes. However, even though you're retired, some of your taxes may actually increase or stay the same. So keep close tabs on the following taxes:

- **Taxes on Social Security benefits:** One tax issue worth paying close attention to in retirement is the triggering of taxes on Social Security benefits if your income exceeds particular thresholds. You also may get socked with higher taxes if you begin collecting Social Security benefits before full retirement age and you're still earning income above a specific threshold. If you can reduce your income below the thresholds, you can save a lot on taxes.

If you're working part time in retirement, you may want to consider contributing to a retirement account to reduce your taxable income.

When investing your money, be sure to pay close attention to your tax situation and select investments that match your tax status.

- **Property taxes:** If you're a homeowner, these taxes are a significant item. Many communities offer some seniors the ability to postpone property tax payments and offer reduced tax rates for lower-income seniors. To qualify, you typically have to present a copy of your completed Internal Revenue Service (IRS) Form 1040 each year.

Housing

Many retirees benefit from the fact that they no longer have mortgage payments in retirement. To manage and even reduce your housing expenses during retirement, you have several options:

- **You may choose to downsize or move to a lower-cost area.** If you live in a high-cost urban or suburban area, after the kids are grown and out in the world, you may choose not to pay higher property taxes and have so much money tied up in a home.

Before you call the moving company, don't resign yourself to being forced to move for financial reasons. If you want to stay in your current home because you like the community, neighbors, local service providers, and area amenities, see what property tax reduction programs your town or city offers to seniors.

- **You may reduce household expenditures for services.** With more free time in retirement, you may be able to reduce some expenditures for services such as a gardener, housekeeper, and household maintenance and repair worker.

Don't underestimate the expertise or physical demands of particular jobs. Servicing your furnace unit may not sound like rocket science, but you can damage the unit or hurt yourself if you don't know what you're doing. Likewise, climbing up a ladder to clean out your gutters may sound like an easy way to save some money until you fall off and break some bones.

- **You may consider taking on a tenant to bring in rental income.** A tenant can help you reduce some of your housing expense burdens. Bringing in a tenant is easier and less intrusive if the proposed rental quarters have a separate entrance and are completely separate from the rest of your living quarters.

  It may be worth making a modest investment to configure your living space to allow for such a rental unit. Just be sure not to undermine the property's value by changing it in such a way that makes the home unappealing to potential buyers. Consult some local real estate agents on your proposed project. Also, be sure to check local zoning laws, building codes, and community association rules for limits on renting part of your home.

Renters and owners with mortgages face different issues. The long-term downside to renting is that your rent is exposed to inflation. Here are some strategies for reducing your housing costs as a long-term renter in retirement:

- **Consider shared housing.** Living with others can improve your social life and reduce your costs. Check with your local senior center or senior's group for information, ideas, and contacts.

_____

_____

_____

- **If you're a lower-income senior, explore rent-subsidized senior housing.** The government gives funding directly to apartment owners who lower the rents they charge to low-income tenants. The U.S. Department of Housing and Urban Development can help you in your search for a rent-subsidized apartment and with understanding the income restrictions to qualify. (Visit www.hud.gov/apps/section8 for more information.) Low-rent apartments are available for senior citizens and people with disabilities as well as for families and individuals. Your state or locality also may have additional programs providing affordable housing to seniors. Many localities have an Area Office on Aging to help seniors identify programs for which they're eligible.

Utilities and communication

Changing the energy and communication sources you're using in your home isn't a simple matter of course for everyone. However, that doesn't mean you're powerless to reduce your utility bills. Here are some steps you can take:

- **Get an energy audit of your home.** Especially if you've lived in your home for many years, odds are it's not as energy efficient as it could be. Contact your local utility company for an energy audit, which you can generally have done for free. Many local utilities offer special incentive programs for energy upgrades.

- **Improve your home's insulation.** If you own an old home, you can probably improve its insulation at a modest cost.

- **Take advantage of tax credits.** A number of state-specific and federal tax credits are available for energy efficiency improvements. For up-to-date information, check out the Database of State Incentives for Renewables & Efficiency website (www.dsireusa.org), which includes links to all state-based and federal incentives.

- **Upgrade energy-wasting appliances.** You'll have to spend some money on these upgrades, but the payback from energy savings can be quite rapid for the worst energy-guzzling appliances.

- **Slim your water bill.** Unless you have a well on your property, you have a water bill that you can lower. Consider taking water-saving actions such as installing water flow regulators in shower heads and faucets. If you buy bottled water or have it delivered, consider instead installing a water purification system.

- **Address telephone costs.** Over the years and decades, phone service costs have declined. However, some folks can get carried away with the increasing numbers of communication devices, including cellphones and smartphones. Be careful about dropping your home phone service and simply going with cellphone service. Cellphone service may not be as easily referenced by local emergency responders when you call 911. Landline service immediately communicates your physical location when you place a 911 call.

- **Try to bundle your television and Internet with your phone bill.** Most folks find that service providers in their area offer both of these services along with others like phone service. Bundling with one provider can lead to the best deals and pricing. Just be careful not to get locked into a long-term plan you may not be happy with or that has hefty early-termination fees.

Food

During retirement you want to manage how much you spend on food. To avoid spending too much, we offer the following suggestions to help you save money:

- **Prepare more meals at home.** With the extra free time afforded by leaving behind full-time work, some folks find they have the time and energy to prepare more meals at home. An added benefit of eating at home is that you can eat healthier and plan ahead. For example, you can cook a casserole and then eat the leftovers for a couple meals.

- **Buy store brands.** The quality and ingredients of store brands are often the same as higher-cost name brands at a much lower price.

- **Eat out for lunch.** Prices usually are less expensive than dinner.

- **Eat out early for dinner.** If you eat dinner earlier, you can qualify for early-bird dinner specials.

- **When you eat out, make two meals out of your purchase.** Most regular servings in restaurants are large enough that you can eat the leftovers at home.

_____

_____

_____

Ask the server to put half of your meal in a take-out container; you can eat it for lunch or dinner the next day.

- **Order off the seniors menu.** Some restaurants offer a discounted seniors menu with smaller portions.

- **Split your meal with a friend.** Some restaurants serve gigantic portions, so ask your server for an additional plate and split your meal with a friend or loved one.

- **Order takeout.** If you enjoy someone else preparing your food without spending a fortune, pick up your meal from your favorite local restaurants.

Transportation

Another benefit of leaving the workforce and retiring is the elimination of work-related transportation expenses. You no longer have a commute and the associated expenses, including gasoline, maintenance, tolls and public transit fees, parking charges, and so on. Your car should last longer too because you likely won't drive as much.

You can further reduce your expenses related to transportation by possibly reducing the number of cars you own. Because you no longer have the burden of daily commutes, you may even be able to make do without a car at all and rely on public transportation. When you need a car for a weekend or other excursion, you can rent one. Some areas also have rent-by-the-hour car rental services for local driving. Getting rid of your car also reduces your auto insurance expenses.

Personal care and fashion

Spending on clothing, shoes, jewelry, dry cleaning, and other amenities also drops when people retire, especially those who worked in more formal office settings. You also will likely spend less on haircuts and salon treatments.

Don't skimp on taking care of your health and being physically active. Consider joining a health club or gym that's user friendly for people of your age and interests. Of course, you don't need a gym membership to be active. Walking, hiking, and other outdoor activities are low cost and generally healthy. Just be careful about falls, which become increasingly common as we age.

Travel and fun

One aspect of retirement you may be looking forward to is the opportunity to travel more. However, be aware that traveling and entertainment aren't cheap. Consider what type of person you are and how your recreation desires may change once you retire.

You may end up spending a bit more on travel and entertainment during your early retirement years compared with later in your retirement years. Most folks don't travel much later in retirement because of reduced mobility and increased health issues. Keep that in mind in the earlier years of retirement and be sure to take advantage of your mobility and money while you're able.

 During your retirement years, you can save money on entertainment and travel expenses in a couple of easy ways:

- **Travel during off-peak times.** You probably have more flexibility as a retiree, so you can travel during the non-busy times and take advantage of cheaper airfares, hotel rooms, and car rental fees.

- **Benefit from reduced senior prices.** You can usually find discounted senior rates at movie theaters, hotels, public golf courses, and other venues. Don't be shy about asking for a senior discount. If you'd rather not inquire when you're at a venue, call in advance and ask about senior rates and who qualifies.

Health care

Most people end up spending more on health care during retirement. The average American over the age of 65 spends about $7,000 per year, and costs keep rising faster than the overall rate of inflation. In your elderly years, even if you remain in good health, you'll probably visit the doctor more and undergo more frequent routine and preventive testing. You also may be surprised at the increase in how much you spend on prescription drugs and dental and vision care visits and procedures.

Insurance

Being able to retire financially is a major milestone. The fact that you're sufficiently financially independent should enable you to reduce and eliminate some insurance, including life and disability insurance. *Note:* One insurance you may need more of is umbrella or excess liability coverage. As your net worth has grown over the years, your need for this coverage grows too. This insurance protects your assets against lawsuits and other liability claims arising from your home and cars.

Children and grandchildren

Having kids grow up and move out of the nest dramatically reduces expenditures related to your kids. Think about all the money parents spend on diapers, day care, toys, sports, music lessons, activities, braces, and so on. If you had kids later in life, or have a special needs child, you may still have some expenses into your senior years. So factor these expenses into your financial plan.

Your grown children and their offspring (your grandchildren) may need or want your financial assistance sometime during your retirement years. If you can afford to help them, consider doing so. But be mindful of keeping them from taking responsibility for their own lives; if they learn that they can always get more money from the First Bank of Mom and Dad, they'll always come around.

_____

_____

_____

4

Retirement Investment Basics

Life is full of choices, and is that ever true when it comes to investments. You have more investments to choose from than you'll ever have time to research.

As you approach and then enter retirement, making smart decisions is more important than ever because you'll likely be living off of your investments. Most people live on their investment income and eventually tap into some of the principal, especially later in their retirement years.

In this chapter, we help you understand investments in general, and then we explain the different types of investments.

Investments Defined

An *investment* is something into which you choose to put your money in the hopes of earning some return and protecting what you've invested. All money, therefore, is in some sort of investment, even what's put in bank accounts, low-return short-term Treasury bills, money market funds, and so on.

As you construct and manage an investment portfolio for your retirement, you must consider numerous factors. You shouldn't, for example, simply chase after investments that historically have posted higher rates of return because those investments tend to be riskier, especially in the shorter term. Also, investments differ from one another in their income-producing ability; how they are taxed; and their sensitivity to inflation, among other factors.

Risk

When you make investments, even low-return ones, you have a potential for *risk*. The risk, of course, is that seemingly attractive higher-return-producing investments can and sometimes do decline in value.

During good economic times, some people make the mistake of feeling as if their money is wasting away or not "invested" if it's in low-return, safer money investments. As a result, they may rush to invest the money elsewhere with the hope of earning a higher return.

Some investments are riskier, which is to say they fluctuate more in value and can produce greater losses over the short term. That's why when you make investments, you need to understand what potentially could happen to your money. You need to consider two important points when considering risk:

- **Risk is fine as long as you understand what you're getting yourself into.** There's nothing wrong with taking risk. In fact, an investor needs to accept risk in order to have the potential for earning a higher return. Just make sure you're educated on the options and understand the risks you're choosing to accept with your choices.

  You need to protect certain types of funds and take little or no risk with them. For example, your emergency reserve fund (which you can tap for unexpected expenses) money shouldn't be in an investment subject to fluctuations in value, such as the stock market.

Instead, you should invest this money in someplace
stable and accessible, such as a savings account or
money market fund.

- **Not taking any risk is risky.** You want to select those
investments that suit your particular goals and your
desire and necessity to take risk, in terms of producing sufficient returns to help pay for your retirement.
The trick is to carefully balance the return you require
against the risk you may be exposed to in seeking a
higher return investment. You need a certain amount of
money saved to maintain a desired standard of living
during retirement. If the money you're accumulating is
invested too conservatively and grows too slowly, you
may need to work many more years or save at a much
higher rate before you can afford to retire. That's why
you should do the number crunching for retirement
planning that we discuss in Chapter 2.

Returns

To fully understand investments, you must keep in mind
that investments differ from one another in terms of their
returns. *Returns* are basically the total profit you earn on

your investment. Investments generally come in two forms:
current income and appreciation.

Current income

Investments may produce *current income*, typically in the
form of interest or *dividends*, which are profits distributed to
corporate stockholders. If, for example, you place your money
in a bank certificate of deposit that matures in one year, the
bank may pay, say, 2 percent interest. Likewise, if you invest
in a Treasury note issued by the federal government, which
matures in two years, you may be paid 3 percent interest.

Income-oriented investments, such as Treasury bills, don't
allow you to profit when the company or organization profits.
When you lend your money to an organization, such as by
purchasing bonds, the best that can happen is that the organization repays your principal with interest.

Appreciation

Some types of investments are more growth oriented and don't
pay much, if any, current income. A *growth investment* is one
that has good potential to *appreciate* (increase) in value in the
years and decades ahead.

Investments that are more growth oriented, such as real estate or *stocks* (investments in companies), allow you to share in the success of a specific company or local economy in general. Some stocks offer dividends as well as the opportunity to participate in the appreciation of stock prices. Although the yield on a good stock from its dividend typically is well below the interest rate paid on a decent corporate bond, some stocks do offer reasonable dividend yields.

Inflation

Some investments are more resistant to *inflation*, or increases in the cost of living. The purchasing power of money invested in bonds that pay a fixed rate of interest, for example, is eroded by a rise in inflation. The value of investments such as real estate, by contrast, often benefits from higher inflation. Stocks, over the long run, have proven to be a good inflation hedge and have produced long-term returns well above the rate of inflation.

Tax consequences

When researching investments, you need to be clear about the possible tax consequences you face with the different investments you may make. Apart from investments in tax-sheltered retirement accounts, the interest or dividends produced by investments are generally taxable in the year they're earned. The profits (known as *capital gains*) from selling an investment at a higher price than it was purchased for also are taxable.

 If you invest without paying attention to taxes, you'll likely overlook ways to maximize your returns. Two simple yet powerful moves can help you to invest in a tax-wise way:

• **Contribute to your retirement accounts so less of your money is taxed in the first place.** Doing so reduces your taxes both in the years you make your contributions as well as each year your money is invested. Consult Chapter 7 for more information on retirement accounts.

• **With money that you invest outside of retirement accounts, choose investments that match your tax situation.** If you're in a high tax bracket, you should avoid investments that produce significant highly taxed distributions. For example, you should avoid taxable bonds, certificates of deposit and other investments that pay taxable interest income, and those that tend to distribute short-term capital gains (which are taxed at the same high tax rates as ordinary income). Instead, consider growth-oriented investments, such as stocks, real estate, or investments in your or someone else's small business. *Long-term capital gains*, which are gains from investments sold after a holding period of more than one year, are taxed at lower rates. Keep in mind that growth-oriented investments generally carry more risk.

If you're in a high tax bracket and would like to invest in bonds outside of a retirement account, consider municipal bonds that pay federally tax-free interest. The interest on municipal bonds is free of state taxes if the bond was issued in the state in which you live.

Sensitivity to economic issues

Not all investments move in concert with the health and performance of the U.S. economy. Investments in overseas securities, for instance, allow you to participate directly in economic growth internationally as well as diversify against the risk of economic problems in the United States. However, even international securities are susceptible to currency-value fluctuations relative to the U.S. dollar.

Because foreign economies and currency values don't always move in tandem with those in the United States, investing overseas may help to dampen the overall volatility of your portfolio. Investing in U.S. companies that operate worldwide serves a similar purpose.

Investment Types

If you're ready to take a closer look at which investments are best for you or if you want to modify your investments to better meet your needs, you've come to the right place. Getting your investment portfolio in order with your money in the right vehicles is an important step to prepare for retirement. To help you settle on the best investments for your situation, we discuss the major types of investments and when you should consider using them.

Lending investments versus ownership investments

Investors are often bewildered at all the investment options from which they can choose. But we can simplify things for you. All the investments you may choose from fall under one of the following two categories:

- **Lending investments:** A lending investment is an investment where you lend your money, typically to an organization. For example, when you place your money in a bank account, such as a savings account, you're essentially lending your money to a bank for an agreed upon interest rate.

   Bonds, which are IOUs issued by companies, are another common lending investment. When you buy a newly issued ten-year bond from Verizon at 6 percent, for example, you're lending your money to Verizon for ten years in exchange for 6 percent interest per year. If things go according to plan, you'll get your 6 percent interest annually, and you'll get your *principal* (the original investment) back when the bond matures in a decade.

- **Ownership investments:** With ownership investments, you own a piece of an asset that has the ability to produce profits or earnings. *Stocks,* which are shares of ownership in a company, and real estate are ownership investments.

  In a capitalistic economy, individual investors build greater wealth by being owners, not lenders. For example, say Verizon doubles in size and profits over the next seven years. As one of its bondholders, you won't share in the growth. As a stockholder, however, you would benefit from a stock price driven higher by greater profits. Ownership investments can also produce income, such as the dividends paid on some stocks or the rental income produced when you rent out real estate.

Over the past two centuries, U.S. stock market investors (owners) have earned an average of 9 to 10 percent per year whereas bond investors (lenders) have earned just 5 percent per year.

Risk and return generally go hand in hand. If you seek safe investments — investments with low volatility and low likelihood of the value of the investment declining — you'll usually have to settle for lending investments with relatively low returns. If you seek higher returns well ahead of the rate of inflation, on the other hand, you must use investments that provide an ownership stake and could either rise or fall in value.

Stocks

Investing in stocks is one of the most accessible ways you can invest for long-term growth. Stocks historically have produced returns averaging about 9 to 10 percent per year. At that rate of return, even without adding to your investment, your money should double every seven to eight years. Thank the rule of 72 for this doubling. The *rule of 72* says that if you divide 72 by your annual return, you'll determine about how many years it takes to double your money.

When companies go *public,* they issue shares of stock that can be bought on one of the major stock exchanges, such as the New York Stock Exchange. As the economy grows and companies grow with it and earn greater profits, stock prices generally follow suit. Stock prices don't move in lock step with earnings, but, over the years, the relationship is pretty close. In fact, the *price-earnings ratio* — which measures the level of stock prices relative to (or divided by) company earnings — of U.S. stocks has averaged approximately 15 during the past century. Although the ratio has varied and crept above 30 and gone as low as 6, it tends to fluctuate around 15.

Be forewarned that the U.S. stock market, as measured by the Dow Jones Industrial Average, has fallen more than 20 percent about every six years. That's the bad news. The good news is that these declines lasted, on average, less than two years. So if you can withstand declines over a few years, the stock market is a terrific place to invest for long-term growth.

 If you're investing in stocks, keep the following two suggestions in mind to help you build wealth faster in the stock market:

- **Reduce fees and commissions while investing.** Not only does excessive trading lead to your possibly being out of the market on the best days and reduce your returns, but it also can increase your transaction costs and taxes. A simple way to stack the stock market odds in your favor is to minimize fees and commissions when investing. That means after you make an investment, you must resist the urge to buy and sell, which raises your fees and commissions. All things being

equal, lower commissions and fees paid to purchase
and hold investments increase your investment returns.

- **Regularly save and invest.** Thanks to the miracle of
compounding, if you save and invest $5,000 per year in a
tax-deferred account returning an average of 10 percent
per year, you'll have about $440,000 in 20 years.

Mutual funds and ETFs

Mutual funds and exchange-traded funds (ETFs) are ideal
investment vehicles to help you carry out your investment
plans. *Mutual funds* are pools of money from investors that a
fund manager uses to buy stocks, bonds, and other assets.

Exchange-traded funds (ETFs) are similar to mutual funds in
that they also invest investors' money into stocks, bonds, and
so on. The difference is that to invest in an ETF, you must buy
it through a stock exchange where ETFs trade.

The three main advantages of the best mutual funds and
ETFs are

- **Diversification:** Mutual funds and ETFs typically invest
in dozens of securities. A truly diversified stock fund
invests in stocks in different industries and different

stocks within an industry. The same logic works for bond funds too.

- **Efficiency:** Good money managers don't come cheaply. However, because funds buy and sell large blocks of securities and typically manage hundreds of millions or billions of dollars, the cost of their services is spread out.

- **Professional oversight:** Unless you have lots of money and free time on your hands, researching investments will, at best, be a part-time hobby for you. A fund manager and her team of analysts are devoted full time to selecting investments and monitoring them on an ongoing basis.

The best mutual funds offer a low-cost, professionally managed way to diversify your investment dollars. *Index funds*, which are a type of mutual fund, invest to follow a specific stock or bond market index and usually have the advantage of low costs, which helps boost your returns. ETFs are generally index-like funds that trade on a stock exchange.

_____

_____

_____

Several different types of funds exist. Which ones work for you depends on the level of risk you desire and can accept. Here's a list of the types you may choose:

- **Money market funds:** These funds are the safest types of mutual funds. Money market funds seek to maintain a fixed share price of $1 per share. They invest in short-term debt of companies and governments. You make your money from the dividends, just like you would with a bank savings account's interest. The main difference and advantage that the best money market funds have over bank savings accounts are that the better ones generate a higher yield or rate of return. Because there's little, if any, risk of bankruptcy, money funds aren't insured the way bank accounts are.

- **Bond funds:** The attraction of bond funds, diversified portfolios of bonds, is that they pay higher dividends than money market funds. So for retirees who want more current income on which to live, bond funds can make sense.

  The drawback or risk of bonds is that they fluctuate in value with changes in interest rates. If the overall level of interest rates rises, the market value of existing bonds decreases. This occurs because with new bonds being issued at higher interest rates, the price of existing bonds must decrease enough that the resulting yield or interest rate is comparable to that offered on new bonds. Longer-term bonds are more volatile with changes in interest rates because your principal is being repaid more years down the road.

The value of bonds issued by corporations also may fluctuate with the financial fortunes of the company. When a company hits a hard patch, investors question whether their bonds will be repaid and drive the price down.

- **Stock funds:** Stock funds invest in shares of stock issued by companies. Most funds invest in stocks of dozens of different companies. Funds typically focus on either U.S. or international companies.

Stock funds are the most volatile of mutual funds and ETFs, but they also hold the promise of higher potential returns. On average, stocks have returned investors about 10 percent per year over the decades. Over short periods, however, stocks can drop significantly in value. Drops of more than 10 or 20 percent aren't uncommon and should be expected. So don't commit money to stock funds that you expect to need or use within the next five years. Although they're completely liquid on a day's notice, you don't want to be forced to sell a stock fund during a down period and possibly lose money.

You can choose to invest in stocks by making your own selection of individual stocks or by letting a mutual fund manager do the picking and managing. Researching individual stocks can be more than a full-time job.

Over the years, increasing numbers of investors have turned to mutual funds for their stock market investing rather than picking and choosing individual stocks on their own. While there's plenty of debate about the merits of these two investment strategies, plenty of sources are pushing investors to individual stocks. For instance, many websites, financial magazines, and television programs advocate for individual stocks.

Investments and their risks

When considering how you want to invest or when studying your current investments, take a close look at the breakdown of the different types you have and their associated risks.

Different combinations can give you different results. Consider these points:

- **Bonds and savings-type vehicles, such as money market mutual funds, deserve a spot in your portfolio.** For money that you expect to use within the next couple of years or for money that you need to earn a relatively high current income from, bonds and money market funds can make great sense. Historically, such investments have produced returns about the same as to a bit more than the rate of inflation (3 percent).

- **Although stocks and real estate offer investors attractive long-term returns, they can and do suffer significant short-term declines in value.** Just consider what happened in the late 2000s severe stock market and real estate decline. These investments aren't suitable for money that you may want or need to use within the next five years.

- **Money market and bond investments are good places to keep emergency money that you expect to use sooner.** Everyone should have a reserve of money that he or she can access in an emergency. Keeping about three to six months' worth of living expenses in a money market fund is a good start. Shorter-term bonds or bond mutual funds can serve as an additional, greater (than money funds) income-producing emergency cushion.

- **Bonds can provide useful diversification for longer-term investing.** For example, when investing for retirement, placing a portion of your money in bonds helps to buffer stock market declines. When investing for longer-term goals, however, some younger investors may not be interested in a significant stake (or any stake at all) in boring old bonds. The reason: They have decades until they will tap their money and are comfortable with the risks of higher returning investments like stocks and real estate.

5

Build a Retirement Portfolio

You may want to put together a solid investment portfolio that will allow you to retire in comfort, but you're wondering how to begin. This chapter can help you get started. We recommend some of our favorite investments and explain how to evaluate, make changes to, and monitor your portfolio.

What You Need to Do Before You Select Investments

In this section, we discuss the importance of matching your financial needs, now and in the future, against the riskiness of your investments. Lastly, we discuss how to whip up the best investment mix — or *asset allocation* — for your situation.

You may already have money invested in a retirement account. Even so, you can still use the information we provide in this chapter to improve upon your holdings and learn from past mistakes.

Know your time horizon

A critical issue to weigh when investing a chunk of money toward a specific goal like retirement is your *time horizon*, or the length of time you have in mind until you need the money.

The potential problem with timing is this: If you invest your money in a risky investment and it drops in value just before you need to sell, you could be forced to take a loss or a much lower gain than you anticipated. So you should be concerned about matching the risk or volatility of your investments with the time frame you have in mind.

Suppose you're investing some money that you plan to use for some one-time expenses in a few years. With a short time frame in mind, investments such as stocks or real estate wouldn't be appropriate because they can fluctuate a great deal in value from year to year. These more growth-oriented (and volatile) investments, on the other hand, can be useful in working toward longer-term goals, such as retirement, that may be a decade or more away. (Chapter 2 provides information on how to figure out when you can afford to retire.)

Factor risk into your investment plan

In addition to the time horizon we discuss in the preceding section, your need to take risk also should be factored into your investment decisions. If the money you're investing for retirement grows too slowly, which may happen if you stash it all in bank accounts and Treasury bills, you may not be able to retire when you want or live the lifestyle you desire. To reach your retirement goals, you may need to take more risk.

Although your retirement goals may require you to take more risk, you don't necessarily have to. Retaining a balanced portfolio of stocks and bonds where you have appreciation potential from the stocks and more income and less volatility from bonds sounds good in theory. But, if you're going to be a nervous wreck and follow the stock market's every move, it may not be worth it for you to take as much risk. In that case, you need to rethink your goals.

Also, if you're in the fortunate position of not need-ing to take much risk because you're well on your way toward your retirement savings goal, taking more risk than necessary may cause you to lose what you have accrued. (Chapter 2 provides more on retire-ment planning.)

Keep the bigger picture in mind

When purchasing a new investment, make sure you consider your overall financial plan. Investors often read articles or get tips from colleagues and wind up buying the recommended investments. Investing without doing sufficient homework leads to a hodgepodge portfolio that's often not properly diversified, among other problems. Failure to make an overall plan usually results in failure, not success.

For example, some investors keep excess cash in low-interest money market funds or savings accounts while they carry high-cost debts, such as auto loans and credit card balances. A better strategy is to pay down the high-cost debt with those excess funds. (This same logic holds for older, more conservative investors who need to pay down mortgages.)

Likewise, some investors who prefer individual stocks worry when one of their holdings falls. Because such investors don't necessarily examine their portfolio's overall performance, they often dump a stock currently in the hole. They dwell on that stock's large decline and overlook how little impact this one holding has on their overall portfolio.

Allocate your assets

When you're investing for longer-term financial goals such as retirement, be sure to invest in an array of different investments. Diversified investments may include such things as stock mutual funds (both U.S. and international), bonds, and, perhaps, real estate.

How you divide your money among these different types of investments is known as *asset allocation.* Asset allocation need not be complicated or intimidating. As a general rule, you should conduct asset allocation for money invested for the longer term — that is, at least more than five years, though preferably ten or more years. See our advice for determining an appropriate asset allocation in Chapter 2.

Before you begin the process of allocating your assets, make sure you have an emergency cash reserve of three to six months of living expenses. Set aside even more if your income and job are unstable and you don't have family or friends you could tap for help. Three months' worth of living expenses, on the other hand, is sufficient if your income is safe and stable or you have other resources you can easily tap.

Other investments that you hold outside of retirement accounts, such as stocks, bonds, and mutual funds that invest in stocks and bonds, can quickly be converted into cash. However, the problem with considering these investments for emergencies is that because they fluctuate in value, the selling price may be much less than what you paid originally.

Managing Your Portfolio

When saving money for your retirement, ultimately you must select investments into which you place that money. Many people find selecting investments stressful and challenging. We're here to remove the anxiety and help you assemble an all-star investment portfolio that will build and protect your wealth over the years ahead.

In Chapter 4, we discuss the spectrum of available investments and highlight the important differences among them.

Ownership investments, including stocks, real estate, and small business, offer the greatest potential returns but also higher risk.

We don't discuss real estate and small business in more detail in this section except to say that for asset allocation purposes, they can fulfill a role similar to investing in stocks.

In this section, we discuss core funds — such as funds of funds, target-date funds, index funds, and exchange-traded funds — that make sense for you to consider. We also present some methods for assessing and managing your investment portfolio.

Funds of funds and target-date funds

Most fund investors feel overwhelmed by having so many choices. They understand the need to hold a diversified portfolio, but they're not sure how to assemble one. Enter fund of funds and target-date funds. Both of these types of funds give you exposure to numerous funds within a single fund. Target-date funds gradually adjust the risk of a portfolio as you approach a particular retirement date.

Funds of funds

Decades ago the mutual fund industry was beginning to reach critical mass and developing and expanding its fund offerings. The large fund companies soon had dozens of funds, and increasing numbers of investors found choosing among them a bit overwhelming.

Informed individual investors understood the concept of diversification and knew they should invest in a variety of funds that gave them exposure to different types of assets. And fund company representatives often found themselves being asked by investors for advice about what basket of funds they should invest in. So, fund companies created *funds of funds* — that is, single funds comprising numerous companies' funds.

For example, consider the Vanguard Star fund. It's made up of 11 Vanguard funds, including domestic and foreign stock funds, bond funds, and a money market fund. Stocks comprise about 62.5 percent of the fund (and about one-fourth of those are foreign), bonds about 25 percent, and money market assets about 12.5 percent. For investors seeking global diversification and an asset allocation similar to this fund's, Star offers low costs (its annual operating expense ratio is just 0.32 percent) and relatively low minimum investment amounts ($1,000).

In addition to the asset allocation, expenses, and riskiness of any fund of funds you may consider, also be sure to consider the tax appropriateness of the fund. Funds of funds that invest in bonds usually aren't very tax friendly because they hold taxable bonds. Therefore, such funds generally only make sense inside a retirement account or for lower-tax-bracket investors investing outside of a retirement account.

Target-date funds

Target-date funds are funds of funds with a twist. Rather than maintaining a generally fixed asset allocation, especially between stocks and bonds, target-date funds adjust their mix over time.

For example, the T. Rowe Price Retirement 2030 Fund is designed for investors expecting to retire around the year 2030. It invests in about 16 different T. Rowe Price stock and bond funds. Over time (and as you approach the retirement date of 2030), the fund reduces its stock exposure and increases its bond exposure. Thus, it reduces the riskiness of the portfolio.

The risks of target-date funds are similar to funds of funds. The only additional risk of a target-date fund is if the fund manager tries to time the markets in his moves into and out of stocks and bonds and guesses wrong. The funds we recommend in this chapter don't suffer this flaw.

_____

_____

_____

Among the better target-date funds we've reviewed include

- Fidelity Freedom funds (www.fidelity.com)
- T. Rowe Price Retirement funds (www.troweprice. com)
- Vanguard Target Retirement funds (www. vanguard.com)

Index and exchange-traded funds

A simple, low-cost way to invest in stocks or bonds is to invest in what's known as an *index fund*. These are passively managed funds that mechanically follow an index, such as one of the following:

- **Barclays Capital U.S. Aggregate Bond Index:** A broad index that tracks the U.S. bond market.
- **Standard & Poor's (S&P) 500 Index:** Tracks 500 large U.S.-headquartered companies' stocks.
- **MSCI U.S. Broad Market Index:** This index follows small, medium, and large U.S.-company stocks.
- **MSCI Europe Index, MSCI Pacific Index, MSCI Emerging Market Index:** These three indexes

respectively track the major stock markets in Europe, the Pacific Rim, and in emerging economies, such as Brazil, China, India, and so on.

- **FTSE All-World Index:** A global stock market index.

All index funds aren't created equal. They do have differences, so make sure you closely investigate any funds before you make an investment:

- **Some have higher expenses than others.** Lower costs are generally better when comparing index funds that track the same index (as long as the lower-cost index fund tracks its index well).

- **Some indexes are likely to produce better long-term returns than others.** For example, we aren't fans of investing in the S&P 500 index because it's a capitalization-weighted index. With this type of index, stocks hold a weighting in the index based on their total market value.

  For instance, during the 1990s, the technology sector's stock weighting in the S&P 500 index ballooned from about 6 percent in 1990 to 29 percent by 1999. So, investors buying into an S&P 500 at the end of 1999 had nearly 30 percent of their investment dollars going into pricey technology stocks. The financial sector experienced a similar ballooning in weighting before its steep price drop in the late 2000s.

In addition to traditional index funds, some index funds invest in *value-oriented stocks*, which are those selling at relatively low valuations compared to the companies' financial positions. Value-oriented stocks are far less likely to hold hot sector stocks destined to crash back to Earth. You also can use index funds that invest in equal weights in the stocks of a given index.

Exchange-traded funds (ETFs) are index-like funds that trade on a major stock exchange. The best ETFs have even lower costs than index funds. But plenty of ETFs have flaws, such as higher costs or a narrow industry or small-country investment focus.

Here's a list (in order from bond funds, U.S. stock funds, and then foreign funds) of index funds and ETFs that are our favorites:

- **iShares Barclays Aggregate Bond (AGG):** This ETF invests in investment-grade bonds and follows the Barclays Aggregate Bond Index.

- **Vanguard Total Bond Market Index (VBMFX):** An index mutual fund that follows the Barclays Aggregate Bond Index.

- **Vanguard Inflation-Protected Securities (VIPSX):** This mutual fund, while technically not an index, largely follows the Barclays U.S. TIPS Index of inflation-protected bonds.

- **Vanguard Small Cap Value (VBR):** This ETF tracks the value companies of the MSCI U.S. Small Cap 1750 Index.

- **iShares Russell 2000 Value Index (IWN):** This ETF follows the Russell 2000 Value index, an index of small company stocks.

- **iShares Russell 1000 Index (IWB):** An ETF that invests in the larger company stocks that comprise the Russell 1000 Index.

- **iShares Russell 1000 Value Index (IWD):** This ETF follows the Russell 1000 Value Index, a larger-cap value index.

- **Vanguard Total Stock Market (VTI):** An ETF that invests in small, medium, and large U.S. stocks.

- **Vanguard REIT (VNQ):** This ETF follows the MSCI U.S. REIT Index, which invests in real estate investment trusts.

_____

_____

_____

- **Vanguard FTSE All-World ex-US (VEU):** An ETF that invests globally per the FTSE All-Word ex-US Index, which includes about 2,200 stocks of companies in 46 countries, from both developed and emerging markets around the world.

- **Vanguard Total International Index (VGTSX):** This index mutual fund tracks the MSCI EAFE Index and the Select Emerging Markets Index.

- **iShares MSCI EAFE Index (EFA):** An ETF that invests to replicate the performance of the MSCI EAFE Index.

Assessing and changing your portfolio

Although we advocate doing your homework so you can buy and hold solid investments for the long haul, we support selling when it's appropriate. If you have investments that seem to be doing badly over an extended period of time, try determining why they've done so poorly and look at making changes to your portfolio.

However, when assessing your current holdings, be careful that you don't dump a particular investment just because it's in a temporary slump. Even the best investment managers have periods as long as a year or two during which they underperform. Sometimes this happens when the manager's style of investing is temporarily out of favor. But remember, "temporary" isn't measured in days or months; instead, think one to two years.

 A useful way to evaluate your portfolio once a year is to imagine that everything that you currently own is sold. Ask yourself whether you'd choose to go out and buy the same investments today that you were holding. Determine whether your reasons still are valid for holding your investments.

When you find something inherently wrong with an investment, such as high fees or subpar management, take the loss and make doing so more palatable by remembering the following:

- **Losses can help reduce your income taxes.** You can see immediate tax relief/reduction for nonretirement losses.

- **Consider opportunity cost.** Consider what kind of future return that money could be providing you with if you switched into a better investment.

_____

_____

_____

As you manage your portfolio:

- **Don't become attached to your investments.** Just as we get attached to people, places, and things, some investors' judgments may be clouded due to attachment to an investment. Even if an investor decides to sell an investment based on a sound and practical assessment, his attachment to it can derail the process, causing him to refuse to part with it at the current fair market value. Attachment can be especially problematic and paralyzing with inherited assets.

- **Don't let inertia become a problem for you.** Some people accumulate tens or hundreds of thousands of dollars in checking accounts. These individuals, who amassed their savings from work income, are often fearful of selecting an investment that may fall in value. They know how long and hard they had to work for their money, and they don't want to lose any of it.

_____

_____

_____

6

Retirement Accounts and Their Rules

One of the virtues and drawbacks of living in the United States is that you have plenty of choices . . . sometimes too many. That's certainly the case with the numerous types of retirement accounts and variety of investments; far more options exist here than in just about any other country in the world.

With so many choices, you may be confused about which option is best for you. Selecting the best ones is important because you can end up saving yourself more tax dollars and making more after-tax money in the long run. And whether you're entering retirement or still a decade (or more) away, you need to understand the rules of each type of account so you can not only make good decisions, but also comply with the myriad tax rules.

In this chapter, we discuss the common types of retirement accounts to which you may contribute. We also discuss early withdrawal penalties, beneficiary decisions, transfer and roll-over rules, and borrowing from or against retirement accounts.

Characteristics of Retirement Accounts

Before you can use retirement accounts to your benefit, you first need to understand these accounts, including the advantages to using them and the potential drawbacks. We lay out these pros and cons in the following sections. Keep this important information in mind as you consider the different types of retirement accounts available. (We discuss your options in the section "Different Types of Retirement Accounts" later in this chapter.)

Tax benefits

The main attraction of any retirement account is the tax savings it provides. You generally receive upfront tax breaks on your contributions up to a certain limit. For example, suppose you're able to contribute $1,000 per month ($12,000 per year) into a tax-deductible retirement savings plan. Assuming that between federal and state taxes you're paying about 35 percent in taxes on your last dollars of income, you should see your federal and state tax bills decrease by about \$4,200 (\$12,000□0.35). This immediate savings is usually enough of an incentive to encourage folks to build wealth by funding retirement accounts.

Because the money contributed to the retirement account isn't taxed at the federal or the state level in the years in which the contributions are made, your take-home pay shrinks by much less than the \$1,000-per-month contribution. Unfortunately, directing money into retirement accounts doesn't allow you to avoid current Social Security and Medicare taxes on wages you earn during the year.

These upfront tax breaks are just part of the value derived from using retirement accounts. You also can reap these other tax-related benefits when you invest in a retirement plan:

- **Your investment returns accumulate without taxation.** After you contribute money into a retirement account, any accumulated investment returns aren't taxed in the year earned. So in addition to reducing your taxes when you make your contribution, you save from this tax-deferred compounding of your investment over time. In other words, all the taxes you would have owed over the years compound in your account and make your money grow faster. You pay tax on this retirement account money only when you make withdrawals.

- **When you invest, Uncle Sam ends up with less of your money.** If you don't invest money in a retirement account, you start with less money in your pocket because the federal and state governments immediately siphon off some taxes. The longer the money is invested, the more you profit by investing inside a retirement account.

Some people are concerned that if their tax rate in retirement is higher than it is during their working and saving years, then funding retirement accounts could lead to higher taxes. Although this scenario is possible, it's unlikely. Because of the tax-deferred compounding, you should come out ahead by funding your retirement accounts. In fact, your retirement tax rate could increase and you'd still come out ahead.

If your employer matches your contributions or contributes additional money to your account, such as with a company-sponsored 401(k) plan, you'll be even better off. Free employer money further enhances the upfront tax benefits by giving you more money working for you.

Restrictions and penalties

Some people contribute little or no money to retirement accounts because of worries about having access to their funds. Although investing your money in a retirement account may limit your access to the money in the short term, overall the investment is a smart move for your retirement in the long run.

If you have to withdraw your money from a retirement account before reaching age 59½, you may incur a tax penalty. The penalty is 10 percent in federal taxes plus whatever penalty your state assesses. This penalty tax is in addition to the regular income tax that's due in the year you make the early withdrawal.

Some exceptions do allow you to withdraw retirement account money before age 59½ without penalty (though you'll still owe income taxes):

- **Five years of withdrawals:** You may withdraw retirement account money early as long as you make withdrawals for at least five consecutive years or until age 59½, whichever is greater. The withdrawals must be substantially equal each year and be based on your life expectancy according to Internal Revenue Service (IRS) assumptions and reasonable interest rates. IRS rulings provide details for computing the annual distributions.

- **Health problems:** If you suffer a disability or incur significant medical expenses, you may be allowed to withdraw money early from your retirement account without penalty. See IRS publication 590 for more information.

- **Borrowing:** Your employer's retirement plan may allow you to borrow from your plan without incurring a penalty. We generally aren't fans of doing this, especially if you seek the money for current spending, such as buying furniture, taking a vacation, and so on. It can make sense, for example, if you need some down payment money to buy a home. But be sure that you understand the repayment rules and terms because if you're unable to repay the loan, the unpaid money is treated as a retirement account withdrawal and subject to current federal and state income taxes as well as penalties unless you withdrew the money after age 59½.

The best solution for short-term money needs is to ensure that you maintain an emergency fund (three to six months' worth of living expenses) outside of your retirement account.

_____

_____

_____

If you don't have an emergency fund, you may be able to borrow money from other sources, such as a family member or through a line of credit or lower-interest credit card.

Different Types of Retirement Accounts

Different employers and employment situations present unique retirement account options. In this section, we explain the common retirement accounts you may be offered and how they work.

Employer-sponsored retirement accounts

When you work for a company or organization, you may have access to an employer-sponsored retirement savings plan. In this case, the company provides access to an investment firm through which you can contribute money via payroll deductions. Plans have rules specifying, for example, how long after becoming an employee you must wait to begin participating in the plan, company matching contributions, and the overall limits of how much you may contribute to your account.

With this type of plan, your employer has done the legwork and maintenance for the plan. However, you're at your employer's mercy if it doesn't have a good plan.

For-profit companies may offer 401(k) plans. Nonprofit organizations can offer 403(b) plans. Government employees may have their own plans such as a 457 plan for state and local government workers and the Thrift Savings Plan for federal government employees. These plans are similar in that contributions into them from your employment earnings aren't taxed at either the federal or state level.

For tax year 2017, the annual contribution limits for these retirement accounts are the lesser of 20 percent of an employee's salary to a maximum of $18,000. If you're 50 or older, your contribution limit is $24,000.

Self-employed retirement savings plans

Another type of retirement plan is the self-employed retirement savings plan. One of the biggest benefits of earning self-employment income is the ability to establish a tax-sheltered retirement savings plan. These plans not only allow you to contribute more than you likely would be saving on a tax-deferred basis for an employer, but they also can be tailored to meet your specific needs.

As with other retirement savings plans, your contributions to self-employed savings plans are excluded from your reported income and are thus exempt from current federal and state income taxes. The earnings that accumulate on your savings over time also are exempt from current income taxes. You pay taxes on your contributions and earnings when you withdraw them, presumably in retirement when you're likely in a lower tax bracket.

A Simplified Employee Pension-Individual Retirement Account (SEP-IRA) is relatively easy to set up and administer. You must establish a SEP by the end of the tax year (usually December 31), but you have until the filing of your federal tax return to make your contribution to the plan. When you as the employer establish a SEP, you must offer this as a benefit to employees if you have them. Speak with a tax advisor or an investment management company for more information.

You may contribute up to the lesser of 25 percent of your self-employment income to a maximum of $54,000 for tax year 2017. To determine the exact maximum amount that you may contribute from self-employed income, you need to have your completed Schedule C tax form so you know your business's net income for the year.

Individual Retirement Accounts (IRAs)

What if you work for an employer that doesn't offer a retirement savings plan? You can lobby your employer to offer a plan, especially if it's a nonprofit, because little cost is involved. Absent that, you can consider contributing to an Individual Retirement Account, or IRA. You may contribute up to $5,500 per year as long as you have at least this much employment (or alimony) income. Those folks who are age 50 and older may contribute up to $6,500 annually.

Whether you can deduct your IRA contribution from your annual taxes depends on whether you participate in another plan through your employer. If you do and your adjusted gross income, or AGI, on your tax return exceeds $62,000 if you file as a single person or $99,000 if you're married filing jointly, the tax deductibility of your IRA is reduced or eliminated.

 If you can't take the tax deduction for a regular IRA, consider a Roth IRA, which allows for tax-free withdrawal of investment earnings in your later years. For tax year 2017, you may contribute up to maximum limits, which are the same as on a regular IRA, so long as your modified adjusted gross income doesn't exceed $118,000 if you're a single taxpayer or $186,000 for married couples filing jointly.

Rolling Over Retirement Balances

One of the most important decisions you'll make with your retirement accounts is what to do with your money in your accounts when you retire. Make the right choice and do the transaction properly, and your after-tax retirement income will be greatly increased. Make a mistake, and you'll pay far more taxes than you need to.

The most common rollover is from a 401(k) plan to an IRA. There are other types of rollovers, however. Money can be moved from one 401(k) to another and from one IRA to another to give two common examples. But the 401(k)-to-IRA rollover is the most common and probably the most important. In this section, as an example, we focus on the important (and common) decision of how to handle a 401(k) account balance when leaving an employer.

What road to take

You should begin planning what to do with your 401(k) account balance well before you leave the sponsoring employer to ensure that you have sufficient time to research and get comfortable with what you're going to do with your money. Too many people make their plans for travel and other activities for the first six months of retirement, but they give no thought to what to do with their 401(k) balances until presented with their options as they're leaving the job.

Most 401(k) plans offer several options for handling an account balance when you leave your employer. Here, we discuss those options and the issues to consider for each one:

- **Leave the balance in the plan until distributions begin.** This option can be a good idea when you like the plan because of its investment options, low costs, or other features. The plan also may allow you to take loans from the account, which could make the plan a source of emergency cash.

However, depending on your circumstances, you may not want to leave your money in the plan for several reasons. For example, you will have more investment options by rolling the balance into an IRA. In addition, the employer could increase fees and change plan offerings between the time you quit and the day you begin receiving distributions. As a former employee, you'll be out of the information loop and may learn about important changes long after current employees. Because of rules and restrictions, most 401(k) plans also are less flexible about post-retirement distributions than IRAs.

- **Look into annuity options.** The plan may offer an annuity option, making fixed, guaranteed payments to you for life or for a period of years, which can be attractive. Look at all your options, though; you may find higher payments available through commercial annuities purchased through an IRA.

When your employer offers an attractive annuity but you don't want the entire account turned into an annuity, you can purchase the annuity with part of the account. The annuity portion can be distributed directly to you, and then taxes are paid only as annuity payments are received. The rest of the account can be rolled over to an IRA.

- **Take the account balance in a lump sum payment.** The entire lump sum would be included in gross income, but the tax law provides a special ten-year income averaging treatment that reduces the tax. You may choose this option when you need or anticipate needing the cash to pay expenses within a few years. Otherwise, you probably should take advantage of tax deferral by leaving the balance in the 401(k) plan or rolling it over to an IRA.

- **Roll over the balance to an IRA.** A *rollover* basically is taking the money from the 401(k) account and moving it to an IRA. The rollover transfers the account to the broker or mutual fund company of your choice for the best combination of fees, investment choices, and other services.

Choosing a custodian and rolling over your balance to an IRA

After deciding that you want to roll over your 401(k) balance to an IRA, determine who will be the IRA custodian. The *custodian* is a broker, mutual fund firm, bank, insurance company, or other financial services company that offers IRAs. When considering which custodian to choose, consider the following (check out Chapter 5 for more details):

- **Research the fees, services, and investment options.** Look for an IRA custodian that has the features and services you desire. You should have an idea of how the account will be invested initially and which types of investments are most important to you.

- **Decide how you will transact most of your business.** Do you prefer talking on the telephone or using the web? Large custodians offer both of these options, but smaller ones may not.

After you select your custodian, you have two ways to roll over a retirement account balance:

- **Option 1:** The trustee for your employer's plan can issue a check to you or make a direct deposit into your bank account. You have 60 days to deposit the check (or an equivalent amount) into an IRA or other qualified retirement plan. If you fail to make the transfer within 60 days, you'll owe income taxes; and if you're under age 59½, you may owe a 10 percent early distribution penalty.

This type of rollover has a trick. When the check is made out to you, the trustee must withhold 20 percent of the account balance for income taxes. The taxes will be refunded to you after you file your tax return and show that you rolled over the account balance within 60 days. But you must deposit in the IRA the entire 401(k) account balance, not only the amount distributed to you. As a result, you must come up with an amount equal to the 20 percent that was withheld and roll that into the IRA along with the amount that was distributed.

- **Option 2:** The other form of rollover is the trustee-to-trustee transfer. The 20 percent withholding isn't required when the distribution check is made payable to a specific IRA custodian instead of to you.

Here's how this easy transaction works:

1. **You open an IRA with the custodian of your choice.**
2. **You complete a rollover form giving the details of the account you want the balance rolled over from.**
3. **The IRA custodian contacts the trustee of your 401(k) plan and ensures that the 401(k) trustee transfers your account balance to the custodian.**

This method is the easier and safer way to roll over your IRA because it avoids the possibility of missing the 60-day deadline of the other method. All you have to do is be sure the 401(k) balance is transferred to your IRA. Sometimes a mistake is made and the transfer is made to a taxable account instead of an IRA. If this isn't corrected promptly, you will owe income tax on the entire amount.

Why would anyone choose Option 1 when they can avoid the hassle of rounding up the extra cash by choosing Option 2? Some employees choose Option 1 because they don't know better and their employers don't warn them before issuing the check. You've now been informed and won't make that mistake.

No matter which of the preceding options you choose, to be tax free a rollover must qualify as a *lump sum,* which means that the entire account must be distributed within the same calendar year. Sometimes a rollover doesn't qualify as a lump sum because some late dividends or other distributions aren't distributed until after December 31. In addition, the employee must be either *separated from service* of the employer (in other words, no longer working for the employer) or over age 59½.

If your 401(k) account contains employer stock, don't transfer the entire account to an IRA. Doing so causes you to lose a valuable tax benefit. When the employer stock is distributed to a taxable account, taxes are generally deferred on it until the stock is sold from that account. In this situation, you maximize tax benefits by splitting off the employer stock from the retirement account. Have the employer stock distributed to a taxable (nonretirement) account and the rest of the account rolled over to an IRA.

Beneficiaries

When you create a retirement account, you need to make sure you select the *beneficiaries* who receive the proceeds. Your will doesn't determine who inherits your IRA and other qualified retirement plans. The account is inherited by whoever is named beneficiary on the beneficiary designation form on file with the plan custodian or trustee.

When choosing your beneficiary, take the time to select the person (or persons) you want to receive your money. Oftentimes people don't give much thought to this important designation. Most people simply write down an obvious beneficiary when they open the account and don't give much thought to it again. In the meantime, they may have been married or divorced or had children or grandchildren. The account probably has grown into a significant asset over time, yet the beneficiary choice hasn't been reconsidered through all these changes.

You need to give some thought to your beneficiary choice as part of your overall estate plan, and you must review that choice every couple of years. Here are some guidelines:

- **Take care of your spouse first.** Retirement accounts are a significant part of most estates. Married people whose priorities are taking care of their spouses name their spouses as the primary or sole beneficiaries of their accounts. Of course, you also should name *contingent beneficiaries* (those who get the account if the primary beneficiary has passed away) in case your spouse doesn't survive you or passes away while assets are still in the IRA. For most people, the contingent beneficiaries are their children in equal shares. But you can name other contingent beneficiaries, such as other relatives or friends.

- **Be careful about naming a trust.** A *trust* is an arrangement in which a trustee manages property for the benefit of someone else. You may want to name a trust as beneficiary to ensure that, for example, your sibling who knows something about investing manages the IRA until your teenagers are older. A trustee also can control how much is distributed. A trust also allows you to control who receives the amount left after the initial beneficiary passes away. However, you have the potential of losing the tax deferral for the IRA if the beneficiary isn't a natural person. Certain types of trusts carry a limited exception to this rule about natural persons. In this case, however, the trust must be carefully written by an experienced estate planner to avoid losing the tax deferral.

- **Consider splitting your IRA.** When you have children but no surviving spouse (or your spouse will have significant non-IRA assets), your children likely will be named equal beneficiaries of your IRA. When children inherit IRA funds, annual distributions are required based on the life expectancy of the oldest beneficiary. The children also must agree on investments and distributions that exceed the minimum required distributions.

Your children have the right to split the IRA into separate IRAs for each of them. You may want to split the IRA now instead of waiting for the kids to work things out. This split gives you more control over the amount of assets each child inherits. It also allows you to name different contingent beneficiaries for each IRA. If you want a trust to control the inheritance of only one beneficiary, splitting the IRA makes this easier. Otherwise, the other beneficiaries have to coordinate their management of the IRA with the trustee.

• **Make charitable gifts with the IRA.** All of your beneficiaries could receive more after-tax wealth when charitable gifts are made with the IRA and other heirs inherit other assets.

Don't name your estate as a beneficiary. A natural person must be beneficiary in order for the IRA to retain its tax deferral. Name your estate as beneficiary, and the IRA must be distributed on an accelerated schedule. Also, don't fail to name a beneficiary; otherwise your estate will be considered the beneficiary.

_____

_____

_____

Required Minimum Distributions

The main purpose of investing in an IRA or other qualified retirement plan is to help you financially during your retirement years. As a result (and because it wants to collect taxes), the federal government requires that you start taking distributions at a certain age. You must begin annual *required minimum distributions* (RMDs) from IRAs and other qualified retirement plans by April 1 of the year after you turn age 70½.

The following sections help you calculate your RMD with an IRA and with other types of retirement accounts.

The RMD is a floor, not a ceiling. You're free to withdraw as much in excess of the RMD as you want. An excess distribution doesn't result in any credit the following year. The adjustment is automatic because the next year's RMD is computed using the account balance as of the end of the current year.

Calculating your RMD for an IRA

To calculate your RMD, you can do the following:

1. **Start with your IRA balance as of December 31 of the year before you turn 70½.**

2. **Divide this amount by your life expectancy.**

   The result of dividing your IRA balance by your life expectancy is your RMD for the year. The good news is you don't have to do the math regarding your life expectancy. Instead you must consult the life expectancy tables in IRS Publication 590 (available free at www.irs.gov). Most people use the "Uniform Lifetime Table."

3. **Repeat the calculation each year.**

   For the first RMD, use the IRA balance as of December 31 of the year before you turned 70½, not the year before the April 1 deadline. The first RMD, though delayed until April 1 of the year after turning 70½, really is the RMD for the previous year. If you wait until April 1 to take the distribution, you'll have to take two distributions in that year: the previous year's distribution, and the current year's distribution that's due by December 31. Taking two distributions in one year could push you into a higher tax bracket. Overall taxes may be lower if the first distribution is taken by December 31 of the year you turn age 70½.

So, for example, if Rick turned 70½ in January 2017 and Corrine turned 70½ in December 2017, each must take his or her first RMD by April 1, 2018. Subsequent RMDs must be taken by December 31 of each year. If you fail to take an RMD, the penalty is 50 percent of the distribution that should have been taken.

When you own more than one IRA, add all the balances together as one to compute the RMD. You can withdraw that amount from the IRAs in any combination you want. Take it all from one account, equally from the different accounts, or in any other way you want. Just be sure that by December 31 your distributions equal (or exceed) the RMD.

If a traditional IRA is converted into a Roth IRA, a new RMD is required for the year of the conversion, using the traditional IRA balance as of December 31 of the preceding year. A new RMD also is required for the year of the IRA owner's death, no matter when during the year that occurred.

Computing the RMD for other retirement plans

All qualified retirement plans — profit-sharing, 401(k), and pension plans — must make RMDs. The basic calculation is the same as for IRAs, but there are some important differences with employer plans.

For employer-sponsored plans (but not for IRAs, SEP-IRAs, and SIMPLE IRAs), the required beginning date is delayed when you're still working for the employer and don't own more than 5 percent of the employer's stock. The first RMD is delayed until April 1 of the year after the year in which you retire.

The calculations for employer plans can be a bit different from IRA calculations. For instance, when you have multiple employer plans, such as a profit-sharing plan and a 401(k) plan, you compute the RMDs separately for each plan instead of totaling them. Check IRS Publication 590 for details (see www.irs.gov).

An employer-sponsored plan can impose stricter rules than the IRS imposes. For example, some employer plans require retired employees to withdraw or roll over their account balances within five years. They may have other stringent restrictions as well. These rules are in the documents describing the employer plan. You're supposed to receive these periodically and can request them at any time from your employer or plan trustee.

7

Guiding Investments and Distributions

As you approach and enter retirement, you'll have plenty of decisions to make regarding your investments. Although some of these are straightforward, others can be quite complex and stressful because you're making decisions that are irrevocable and have long-term consequences.

This chapter should help you minimize that stress and maximize the financial results from these important decisions. In this chapter, we explain how to adjust your investment mix over the years, estimate your investment income, keep your portfolio balanced, assess what roles annuities should play in your retirement plans, choose among your pension options, and plot your retirement account withdrawal strategies.

Guiding Your Investments through Retirement

In Chapter 5, we discuss the importance of developing an overall investment plan known as your *asset allocation*. Although this is important, coming up with a plan isn't enough because you need to manage and adjust your allocations over the years, too. Then, as you approach retirement, you'll likely need to assess how to live off your investments, such as through receiving the investment income from your portfolio. The following sections help you figure out how to manage your allocations and determine how much you need to live comfortably.

Estimate your investment income

Most near-retirees are at least a little frightened at the prospect of losing their employment income and having to live off of their investments and monthly benefit checks (such as Social Security and their pension, if they have one). Even if you don't have to withdraw money from your financial assets at the beginning of your retirement, you may need to later.

Be careful to understand that your investment income may vary. For example, in a severe economic downturn (like the one in the late 2000s), stock dividends and bond interest may be reduced, so give yourself some wiggle room.

Make the calculations

When estimating your investment income, make sure you examine your current investment holdings to determine about how much annual income (not capital gains distributions) those investments are throwing off. Tally that income with your other income to see whether you'll have enough to meet your anticipated annual spending desires or needs. *Note:* Most folks don't feel comfortable tapping into their investment principal, so they seek to use the income from their investments. If you have sufficient assets and those assets are properly diversified, you may be able leave your investment principal intact.

The good news: You can figure out all the numbers and estimate how much money you have by using the relatively simple guidelines, such as the 4 percent rule, that we provide in Chapter 2. These guidelines can help you determine how much of your assets you can safely use each year and have confidence that your money will last as long as you do.

_____

_____

_____

Determine whether to modify your investments to earn more income now

Some people are so opposed to using their investment principal that they are willing to dramatically overhaul their portfolios to be able to live off of the income for a significant number of years. Generally, this isn't a good idea.

Unless you have an unbelievably large amount of principal in your portfolio, you would have to invest in highly risky investment vehicles to achieve the types of returns that would allow you to live off only the income from your portfolio. You would be able to meet your income objectives in the short-term, but over the long-term your portfolio would have no real growth potential.

You may, however, want to modify your holdings if you're coming close to realizing your investment income desires. For example, suppose you have about 65 percent in stocks and 35 percent in bonds. You crunch some numbers and realize that a 50/50 mix will boost your investment income enough to close the gap. As long as that mix makes sense given your overall goals and situation, making a modest shift like this may make sense. Realize, though, the trade-off is that reaching for more current income will likely reduce the longer-term appreciation potential of your portfolio.

_____

_____

_____

Rebalance your investments

Rebalancing is a rather clever system that disciplines you to buy low and sell high. It forces you to get your portfolio's asset allocation back to where it should be. For example, suppose you had a 50/50 mix between stocks and bonds. And then suppose stocks do poorly while bonds do well, so now you've got a 40/60 mix with bonds now in the majority. Rebalancing would have you sell enough bonds and buy more stocks to get back to the original 50/50 mix. In the following sections, we show you why balancing is so beneficial and then illustrate its success with an example.

The benefits of rebalancing

You may ask why anyone would take money from an investment that's doing well (bonds) and put some of that into an investment that's doing poorly (stocks). The reasons are twofold:

- **It helps get your investment plan back on track.** You developed an asset allocation plan and should stick to it unless you have a compelling reason — such as a change in your personal situation — to alter your plan.

- **It allows you to take advantage of the inevitable rebound that stocks should eventually enjoy.** Asset classes, like stocks, that suffer setbacks don't stay down forever.

Here are some important tips to make the most of and be smart about rebalancing:

- **Beware of tax consequences.** If you're selling investments outside of retirement accounts and those sales trigger realized profits, you'll owe taxes on those profits. That's why rebalancing is best done with money inside retirement accounts where you don't need to be concerned with tax consequences on transactions.

- **Beware of transaction costs.** When you buy and sell certain investments, such as individual stocks and bonds, you may incur fees.

  With most exchange-traded funds and no-load mutual funds, this isn't an issue, but it will cost you to trade most other investments. That doesn't mean you shouldn't rebalance if you have to pay some transaction costs; it simply means you should fully understand trading fees before you take action. If transaction costs are involved, you may want to rebalance a little less frequently than you would otherwise.

- **Find ways to rebalance by not making unnecessary trades.** You can avoid transaction and tax costs through rebalancing with distributed investment income (interest and dividends), new contributions, and planned withdrawals.

- **Select a sensible rebalancing period/trigger.** Numerous studies have shown that the benefits don't outweigh the costs when rebalancing is done frequently — such as monthly and quarterly. The best approach is to review your portfolio one or two times per year and rebalance if your investment allocations have moved off base by at least 5 percent.

A rebalancing example

Consider the following example that shows rebalancing in action: Suppose you currently have $100,000 invested for your retirement in an asset allocation of 60 percent stocks and 40 percent bonds. And further suppose that over the next two years, the stocks drop 50 percent in value, while your bonds produce a total return of 10 percent. Table 7-1 shows what will happen to your asset allocation in the absence of any changes from you.

	Starting Mix	Mix after Two Years
Stocks	$60,000	$30,000
Bonds	$40,000	$44,000

Table 7-1: *Allocation Changes*

As you can see from Table 7-1, after two years, instead of having 60 percent in stocks and 40 percent in bonds, you now have about 41 percent in stocks and about 59 percent in bonds. To return to your original chosen allocation, you would need to move about $14,400 out of bonds and into stocks. Refer to Table 7-2 to see what the numbers would look like after the rebalance.

	Starting Mix	Mix after Two Years	Mix After Rebalancing
Stocks	$60,000	$30,000	$44,400
Bonds	$40,000	$44,000	$29,600

Table 7-2: *Allocations After Rebalancing*

Annuities

As we discuss in Chapter 4, you can channel contributions into numerous types of retirement accounts. By directing money into such accounts, you may derive significant tax benefits.

Annuities provide an additional vehicle for saving and investing money in a tax-sheltered fashion. And compared with traditional retirement accounts like IRAs and 401(k)s, annuities offer a unique way of tapping the money within them through *annuitizing* (receiving monthly payments). We discuss these issues in this section.

Annuities: A cross between a retirement account and insurance

Annuities are a bit of a quirky investment vehicle in that they have similarities to some retirement accounts but also have some elements of insurance. Although annuities don't offer upfront tax breaks for contributions, the investment earnings accumulate without taxation, as they do in retirement accounts, until withdrawn.

This is how the insurance feature of an annuity works: If the annuity holder passes away and the annuity account value is lower than the original amount invested, the beneficiaries of the annuity get back the original investment amount.

Here's an example to illustrate: Suppose Alan invested $100,000 in a variable annuity (which is discussed in the following section) and directed much of the money into stock mutual funds. His stock fund investments dropped significantly along with the rest of the global stock markets. When his investments began to bounce back three years later, Alan died. His annuity's account value was $85,000, or $15,000 less than he invested. In this case, his beneficiaries get $100,000 from the annuity, not just $85,000.

Contributing in your working years

If you've maximized contributions to retirement accounts through your employer and an IRA, and you want to put away more money to compound without taxation during your working years, you can consider an annuity. You have a couple of options when investing in annuities:

- **Variable annuity:** With this type, you may invest in mutual funds inside the annuity.

- **Fixed annuity:** This type of annuity pays you a set rate of interest, which is typically adjusted annually at the discretion of the annuity issuer.

People who are comfortable investing in mutual funds should be fine using a variable annuity. On the other hand, if you prefer knowing your return in advance and are willing to accept a likely lower long-term return in exchange for eliminating the downside risk, consider a fixed annuity.

Annuitizing in your retirement years

With fixed or variable annuities, you can *annuitize* the assets. In other words, you can convert them into a monthly income stream during your retirement years. When you annuitize, you enter into an agreement to receive monthly payments in exchange for the total balance in the account.

Under this agreement, you receive monthly payments in one of the following ways:

- **Variable payments:** The monthly income you receive varies with the performance of the investments.
- **Fixed payments:** Under this option, you receive the same amount per month for a certain period of time.

- **A combination:** With this option, a portion of your payment is fixed and a portion can be variable.

If you currently don't have money in an annuity and are approaching retirement, you can immediately put funds into a *lifetime income annuity,* also called an *immediate annuity.* In other words, with your contribution, you immediately annuitize and begin receiving monthly payments. As with annuitizing an existing annuity, lifetime income annuities can provide fixed, variable, or inflation-adjusted monthly income. The choice is up to you.

When you annuitize, you generally have a lot of payment options. The options may vary a bit by annuity provider and by state, but the following are the most common:

- **Period certain:** In this case, you choose a certain number of years (for example, a minimum of 5 years to a maximum of 30 years) over which you're guaranteed to receive monthly payments. The longer the period over which you'd like to get payments, the lower those payments will be. In the event that you pass away before the end of the designated period, your beneficiary receives your remaining payments.

- **Lifetime annuity:** With this option, you receive a monthly check for the rest of your life. Payments cease when you pass away.

- **Lifetime annuity with period certain:** This option provides payments for life, but you're also guaranteed payments for a particular period of time (for example, between 5 years and 30 years). If you pass away before the completion of the period certain payments, your designated beneficiary receives your remaining payments.

- **Joint and survivor annuity:** In this case, monthly payments continue as long as you or your designated annuitant (for example, your spouse) are alive. You have options for the survivor's payments. You may continue the survivor's payments at 100 percent, 75 percent, or 50 percent of your amount. The higher the percentage you desire, the lower your initial payments will be, however.

_____

_____

_____

Pension Options

A *pension plan* certainly simplifies the process of saving for retirement. With such a plan, the employer puts away money on your behalf and invests it on your behalf.

Some employees, especially those who work for larger organizations, earn pension benefits. Slowly but surely, however, such plans are being phased out and replaced by plans like 401(k)s where the employee must elect to save their own money from their paycheck and direct the investment of it over the years. Head to Chapter 6 for more on 401(k)s.

If you're fortunate enough to have a pension plan, you want to make the right decisions to receive distributions during your senior years. With pension plans, you typically face two important decisions:

- You have to decide whether to take the pension as a monthly retirement payment or a lump sum distribution.

- Those who opt for the monthly pension payment usually have a second decision among several payment plan options.

We deal with each of these in turn starting with the first and biggest issue — lump sum or monthly payments.

Lump sum versus monthly payments

The first question you should contemplate when considering your pension options is whether to take a lump sum payment or monthly payments. With a *lump sum payment*, you get one large payment, and with *monthly payments*, you get a set amount per month over an extended period of time.

Like the cost of a house, a lump sum sounds like a big number. However, pension plans offering a lump sum option generally are structured to provide about the same expected value to employees. That's why it's usually difficult to decide based on financial factors; the decision hinges more on qualitative considerations, for example, such as your desire to control and invest the money yourself and have money left over for heirs should you pass away prematurely in retirement.

In making this important decision, beware of financial planners' and brokers' advice when they aren't paid hourly or with a fixed fee. If you take a monthly pension, there's no lump sum for them to manage.

_____

_____

_____

Taking stock of your situation

When deciding between a lump sum and a monthly payment, start by surveying your progress with retirement planning and determining how much risk you can take with your pension money. Prospective retirees should conduct a retirement analysis to determine how the standard of living likely to be provided by their assets compares with their expected retirement expenses.

Key issues regarding your pension decision

After you take stock of your financial situation, you have a few additional considerations to think about when weighing a monthly payment versus a lump sum. Keep these in mind as you make your decision:

- **How adept are you with managing money?** A major benefit of a pension is that the investment responsibility rests with professional pension managers who are far less likely to make dramatic moves. The best way to answer this question is to reflect on your historic experience managing money. If your track record is problematic or you simply lack such experience, lean toward the monthly pension and steer clear of the lump sum.

- **What's your health situation and family longevity record?** If you have a major medical problem or reason to believe that your genes destine you to fewer golden years, one advantage of the lump sum is that you get all the money to use and use sooner if you choose — and you can leave the remainder to your heirs. A monthly pension lasts only as long as you do (with reduced benefits as long as your spouse survives after you).

- **How comfortable will you be tapping into principal?** Many retirees are fine with living off investment income, but it's psychologically difficult for most to use principal. Thus, pension checks, which are more comfortably spent, can provide a higher standard of living.

- **What's the safety of your pension benefits?** Retirees often fear that a pension benefit also may last only as long as a company does. But you don't have to worry; pensions are backed by the Pension Benefit Guaranty Corporation (PBGC), an independent government agency.

Monthly payment options

If you opt for a monthly check, some plans offer options that differ from one another the way that investments do in terms of risk and return. Here's a rundown of the most common options:

- **The 100 percent joint and survivor option:** The "safest" option, with the lowest payment, is the 100 percent joint and survivor option. This payment continues as long as either the pensioner or his or her spouse is still living. This option makes sense for risk-averse retirees who are dependent on the pension check (and perhaps aren't in the best of health) and whose spouses also are dependent on that pension check.

- **The two-thirds joint and survivor plan:** The two-thirds joint and survivor plan is intermediate in risk and payment amount. With this plan, after the death of the pensioner, the survivor receives two-thirds of the pension amount paid to the pensioner before his or her passing.

- **The single-life option:** The riskiest option but the one that maximizes payments now is the *single-life option.* This option makes payments only as long as the pensioner is living. We would advocate selecting this option only if you're in good health, have plenty of assets, and your spouse could afford to live without the pension check.

After you decide you want a monthly check instead of a lump sum, don't automatically take the pension offered by your employer. You may find a better deal from an insurance company annuity. For instance, you can take the lump sum from your employer and use the funds to buy an annuity. Find out the monthly check you would receive from some insurance annuities purchased with the lump sum that you're eligible for. Compare those with the monthly payments offered by your employer. Before opting for an insurance annuity, however, keep financial security in mind. An insurance annuity is backed only by the insurer and perhaps a limited guarantee from a state insurance fund. Your employer annuity is backed by both the pension fund and the PBGC.

Withdrawal Strategies for Your Investment Accounts

To make the most of your money, you should understand the rules and your options regarding withdrawing money from various accounts, both retirement and regular, in your golden years.

Here are some general tips to keep in mind regarding tapping your investment accounts:

- **Tap nonretirement account money first.** All other things being equal, it's generally better to tap your nonretirement holdings first — if you'll experience less of a tax bite by doing so. However, don't assume you'll pay more taxes to tap money inside retirement accounts. That may not be the case if some of that money already has been taxed and if selling nonretirement assets would trigger a big tax bill.

  An exception is when your nonretirement accounts are invested to earn much higher returns than your

retirement accounts, especially when the returns in
the nonretirement accounts will be taxed at favorable
long-term capital gains rates. When the nonretirement
accounts earn 4 percent or more annually than the
retirement accounts, it's better to tap the retirement
accounts first.

- **Let tax-free accounts, such as Roth IRAs, compound
  as long as possible.** Spend from your other accounts
  before tapping a Roth IRA. You'll maximize your
  long-term returns by keeping more money in accounts
  that provide for tax-free accumulation and withdrawal
  of money.

- **Tap your nonretirement accounts efficiently.** Sell
  investments with *paper losses* (those that have gone
  down in value versus their purchase price) first.
  Next, sell assets that will incur the lowest tax bill as a
  percentage of their value. These steps defer taxes as
  long as possible and maximize the amount of after-tax
  wealth available during retirement.

- **Understand bigger picture tax issues.** In addition to
  income taxes, you may have estate tax issues to consider regarding which of your assets you should use.

Spend the money to consult with a competent tax advisor as needed.

- **Use your money!** Too often, retirees who were good savers during their working years have great difficulty enjoying and using their money in retirement. See our discussion in Chapter 1 to calm your fears and worries about possibly running out of money.

_____

_____

_____

8

Social Security

Social Security is one of the least understood components of senior Americans' personal finances. Traditionally, income during retirement comes from a combination of three sources: employer pensions, personal savings, and Social Security. Many Americans generally take Social Security for granted and don't give it much thought.

However, Social Security is quite important as you attempt to get a firm grasp on your personal finances. Too few people take the time to understand the options and the effects of their decisions about Social Security. And most financial advisors know little about Social Security retirement benefits.

That's why we're here: To help you get a better grasp of how Social Security can affect your finances. This chapter focuses on the important decisions involving Social Security retirement benefits and how you can make them.

Although the Social Security program also offers disability and survivor benefits, this chapter focuses primarily on retirement benefits with some attention paid to the survivor benefits of a spouse.

An Introduction to Social Security

Most Americans think that Social Security simply is an automatic payment that begins at retirement and that they have little or no influence over the amount of the payment. In truth, Social Security is a fairly broad and complex program that provides retirement, survivor, and disability benefits. Retirement benefits are not automatic. You choose when they begin, and the choice affects the amount of benefits you receive. The amount of benefits you receive also can depend on your spouse's benefits. You even can change your mind after starting to receive benefits.

The original intent of Social Security's retirement benefits was to provide a basic minimum income for retired workers. The lower your working years' income was, the greater the percentage of that income Social Security would replace. However in recent years, Social Security has undergone some changes, and employers are steadily eliminating *defined benefit pension plans* (those that guarantee a fixed monthly retirement payment for life), shifting the risk of saving and investing to employees. As a result, for many people, Social Security retirement benefits are the only source of retirement income that's both guaranteed and indexed for inflation.

When you decide to begin receiving Social Security benefits determines the amount of the benefits. Other issues also decide the amount of your benefits. The key issues that determine the amount of benefits you receive are

- The age at which you (and your spouse, if you're married) begin receiving retirement benefits
- Whether your benefit payments are based on your work record or your spouse's
- Whether you should change from receiving benefits based on your spouse's earnings record to benefits based on your earnings record, or even change the age at which you begin receiving benefits
- Whether your marital status changed over the years — which could lead to additional choices

You have several opportunities to make choices about your retirement benefits, and the choices greatly influence the amount of payments you'll receive. Because Social Security continues for life, the choices you make can alter lifetime income by tens of thousands of dollars or more. Your decisions also affect the amount of survivor benefits your spouse receives. Your financial security is enhanced if you find ways to increase the guaranteed income from Social Security retirement benefits.

Becoming Eligible for Benefits

You're eligible for Social Security retirement benefits after earning 40 work credits. You earn a *work credit* for each quarter year (three months) in which your earned income, subject to the Social Security tax, exceeded a minimum level. The minimum income level is indexed for inflation and was $1,300 for 2017. Therefore, you're entitled to retirement benefits if you work a total of at least 40 quarters (ten full years) during your lifetime in which you earn more than the minimum amount of income covered by Social Security.

After you know you're eligible to receive benefits, determining the level of benefits you use isn't quite as clear. The benefits are based on the highest 35 years of earnings before beginning benefits. The earnings from prior years are indexed for wage inflation as part of the computation. The result is a figure called *average indexed monthly earnings*, which is used to determine your benefits. This computation is quite technical, but we cover the essentials here; if you're interested in more of the fine details, go to the Social Security website (`www.ssa.gov`).

In general, the higher the income you post for your highest 35 years of working, the higher your benefits will be. However, there's a limit on the amount of income subject to Social Security taxes during your earning years. The benefit computation doesn't include income earned above that limit.

Even though higher-income earners receive more benefits than lower-income earners, the benefits for higher-income earners replace a smaller proportion of earnings than for lower-income earners. In other words, individuals with lower lifetime earnings have a higher replacement ratio than those with higher incomes. The *replacement ratio* is the percentage of working income that's paid in retirement benefits.

Lower-income retirees can receive Social Security benefits equal to about 90 percent of their pre-retirement income. The benefits of high-income retirees are about 15 percent of pre-retirement income.

So how can you figure out when you can start receiving distributions from Social Security and what the benefits would be at different ages? The following two sections can help you make those determinations. If you're not at retirement age yet, your first resource is the annual earnings history report you receive from the Social Security Administration (SSA). You also need to know what Uncle Sam has defined as the age you can retire to receive your full benefits.

Reviewing your earnings history

The SSA generates an annual statement of estimated benefits for every person with an earnings history each year. You can access this statement at www.ssa.gov. The statement shows the earnings history in Social Security's records and estimates the retirement benefits that would be received if benefits were to begin at ages 62, 70, and full retirement age (which for most people still working is around age 66 or 67). Other information and estimates also are included.

The earnings history in the annual statement is critical. If the history is incorrect, the benefits eventually paid to you will be incorrect. You have three years to correct an error in a year's earnings amount. We suggest that you review the recent earnings history each year in your birth month and decide whether it needs to be corrected. If you need to correct it, you can call the SSA at 800-772-1213 from 7 a.m. to 7 p.m. every business day, or you can take your records to your local SSA office. To correct your earnings record, you need to give your name, Social Security number, the year or years that contain erroneous earnings, and the business name and address of your employer in those years. Helpful items to have are your W-2 forms (or tax returns if you're self-employed) for the incorrect years.

An examination of the earnings history can provide useful information to decide what may be a good age for you to retire. Most people have low earnings during the early years of their careers and mostly steadily rising earnings after that. Workers suffering extended layoffs, however, may have low income-earning years at other times in their work histories. Remember that the benefits calculation uses your highest 35 years of earnings, so working a few extra years could remove the lowest earning years from your "high 35" and ultimately increase your Social Security retirement benefits. An increase in the benefits means a higher payment every month for the rest of your life, so it could amount to a large sum over time.

Defining when you can retire

The federal government has set the benchmark for retirement benefits, called *full retirement age* (FRA), or *normal retirement age*. If you begin retirement benefits at this age, you receive *full retirement benefits* (FRB), also known as *normal retirement benefits*. Begin benefits earlier, and you receive lower monthly benefits. Delay receiving benefits after FRA, and you receive a higher annual payment.

For many decades FRA was 65. The reforms of 1983 phased in a higher FRA for anyone born after 1937 (anyone who turns 65 after 2002). When fully phased in, the schedule creates a new FRA of 67 for anyone born after 1959. Check out Table 8-1 for a schedule of FRAs to see where you fall.

_____

_____

_____

Year of Birth	Full Retirement Age
1943–1954	66
1955	66 and 2 months
1956	66 and 4 months
1957	66 and 6 months
1958	66 and 8 months
1959	66 and 10 months
1960 and later	67

Note: If you were born on January 1 of any year, you should refer to the previous year. If you qualify for benefits as a survivor, your full retirement age may be different.
Table 8-1: *Age to Receive Full Social Security Benefits*

There's an annual limit on the amount of retirement benefits, regardless of pre-retirement income. The limit is indexed for inflation. So, for example, someone retiring at full retirement age in 2017 received no more than $2,687 monthly, regardless of how high her lifetime earnings are. (For comparison, the average monthly retirement benefit paid in 2017 was $1,342.)

You can begin receiving Social Security retirement benefits as early as age 62, and you don't have to be retired from work to receive them. You can choose the starting date. However, if you begin the benefits before FRA, the amount of benefits will be reduced below the FRB. The benefit is reduced by a percentage for each month you begin benefits before FRA. The amount of the reduction depends on the year of your birth. The reduction in benefits for early retirement is a little complicated; if you want the details, search for "reduction in benefits" on the SSA's website (www.ssa.gov).

The law provides an incentive, known as *delayed retirement credits*, to delay receiving benefits after FRA. The credits are a rate of increase in your benefits for each month you postpone receiving benefits, and the rate of increase depends on the year you were born. So, your age and the number of months you delay receiving benefits determine how much benefits increase when you wait.

If you were born in 1943 or later, your yearly rate of increase is 8 percent; the monthly rate of increase is ⅔ of 1 percent. There are no increases for delaying benefits past age 70.

A third factor is the salary you receive if you continue to work before receiving benefits. Because your highest 35 years of earnings are used to calculate benefits, working more years may increase your FRB if later higher-earning years push lower-earning years out of the top 35.

Spousal and Survivor Benefits

Many seniors consider more than themselves in financial decisions. They also have spouses to be concerned about, and benefits for a spouse are among the least understood aspects of the Social Security program. Here are the two dimensions to incorporating a spouse in decisions on Social Security benefits:

- A married person can receive either spousal benefits based on the other spouse's earnings record or retirement benefits based on his own work record, whichever results in higher benefits.

- A surviving spouse can receive survivor benefits based on the earnings record of the deceased spouse. Keep in mind that the decision of when to begin receiving your own benefits can affect the amount of survivor benefits received by your spouse.

Note the important difference between the spousal benefit and survivor's benefit: While the higher-earning spouse is alive, the lower-earning spouse's retirement benefit is half of the higher-earning spouse's benefit at FRA (or his own retirement benefit, whichever is higher), regardless of when the higher-earning spouse decided to begin benefits. But after the higher-earning spouse passes away, the lower-earning spouse's survivor benefit is equal to the retirement benefit that the higher-earning spouse was receiving. The amount of the survivor benefit depends on the age when the higher-earning spouse chose to begin benefits. If the higher-earning spouse began receiving benefits before FRA, the surviving spouse will receive less than the FRB as a survivor benefit, and that reduction will continue for the rest of the surviving spouse's life.

We explore these dimensions in detail, because the age at which you decide to begin benefits affects the benefits received by a spouse, a surviving spouse, and even an ex-spouse. We begin with some simple strategies and build to some more sophisticated strategies.

Choices for spousal benefits

One way you can enhance your personal finances as a senior is to take advantage of the spousal benefit. The *spousal benefit* is the amount of retirement benefits a married person is entitled to based on the earnings record of the other spouse. This benefit is different from the *retirement benefit* you're entitled to based on your own earnings history. You may receive either the spousal benefit or the retirement benefit, but not both.

 The Social Security Administration is supposed to automatically compare the spousal benefit to the earned retirement benefit and automatically pay the higher of the two. No action is supposed to be required by a beneficiary to receive the higher benefit. But mistakes can be made, so you should know the benefit you're entitled to and be sure that is what you're receiving. If you aren't, contact the SSA.

If you're the lower-earning spouse, you can start receiving spousal benefits when your higher-earning spouse begins receiving retirement benefits. The two of you have some important decisions to make before the lower-earning spouse takes benefits, however. *Note:* To help you grasp what you and your spouse can do, we assume one spouse has higher lifetime earnings than the other. We refer to the spouses as the *higher-earning spouse* and the *lower-earning spouse.*

In general the spousal benefit is one-half of the benefit at FRA earned by the other spouse, if the lower-earning spouse doesn't begin receiving benefits until her own FRA or later.

However, it doesn't matter whether the higher-earning spouse begins benefits at age 62, age 70, or somewhere in between. The spousal benefit is one-half the benefit that the higher-earning spouse would receive by beginning benefits at FRA. Also, when the lower-earning spouse receives the spousal benefit, it doesn't affect the amount of benefits received by the higher-earning spouse.

So what choices does the lower-earning income spouse have? The following sections explain your options along with some examples.

Choice No. 1: Lower-earning spouse retires first, takes own benefits

When the higher-earning spouse hasn't begun receiving retirement benefits, the lower-earning spouse's only option is to begin receiving retirement benefits based on her earnings history. A spousal benefit can't begin until the higher-earning spouse actually begins receiving benefits. If the lower-earning spouse wants to begin benefits but the higher-earning spouse is delaying benefits, the lower-earning spouse's only option is to receive benefits based on her own earnings record. After the higher-earning spouse begins receiving benefits, the lower-earning spouse can shift to the spousal benefit.

Choice No. 2: Higher-earning spouse retires, boosts lower-earning spouse's benefits

After the higher-earning spouse begins retirement benefits, the lower-earning spouse can choose either a spousal benefit or his own retirement benefit. When the lower-earning spouse is already receiving benefits based on his own earnings history, he can switch to the spousal benefit after the higher-earning spouse begins retirement benefits.

If a lower-earning spouse decides to take benefits based on the higher-earning spouse's earnings record, the lower-earning spouse receives half of the higher-earning spouse's FRB, but only if the lower-earning spouse waits until his own FRA to begin any benefits. If the lower-earning spouse decides to begin benefits (whether his own retirement benefit or a spousal benefit) before his own FRA, the spousal benefit will be less than half of the higher-earning spouse's FRA. The benefit will be reduced on a sliding scale. If the lower-earning spouse selects age 62, he will receive a benefit that's 35 percent of the higher-earning spouse's FRA benefit.

For example, say each spouse is age 62. The lower-earning spouse's earned retirement benefit is $900 monthly at FRA or $500 at 62. The higher-earning spouse is entitled to $1,900 monthly at FRA. The lower-earning spouse wants to begin receiving benefits now. The higher-earning spouse continues to work and delays benefits. The lower-earning spouse begins receiving $500 at 62. The higher-earning spouse finally begins receiving benefits at FRA of $1,900. The lower-earning spouse now can switch to receive half of the higher-earning spouse's benefit. Normally the spousal benefit would be $950 (half of the higher-earning spouse's FRB), but because the lower-earning spouse began receiving benefits at 62 the benefits are reduced by 35 percent. By beginning his own retirement benefits early, the lower-earning spouse permanently reduces monthly benefits, even if he later switches to the spousal benefit.

Choice No. 3: Claim and suspend

You have a third option as a lower-earning spouse. Social Security allows a person to file for retirement benefits and then suspend receipt of them. The suspension is treated as though the person never applied for benefits during the suspension period. The monthly reductions for claiming benefits before FRA aren't applied, and delayed retirement credits accumulate during the suspension period. Once a beneficiary suspends benefits, she can have the benefits resume at any time. If the benefits are applied for at age 62 but suspended until age 70, the maximum benefit may be received at 70.

This is known as the *claim-and-suspend strategy.* The claim-and-suspend strategy can be used to allow the lower-earning spouse to begin receiving a spousal benefit now while the higher-earning spouse effectively delays receipt of benefits and receive higher benefits in the future.

If you're younger than FRA and you continue working for an income exceeding the earned income limit, you don't need to file to suspend the benefits. The adjustment process automatically is done through the earnings test. Benefits are reduced if you earn too much money while receiving benefits before FRA, but the reduction increases benefits received later. But at FRA and later, a beneficiary must apply to suspend the benefits.

Survivor's benefits

If you're the higher-earning spouse, you want to make sure your lower-earning spouse is taken care of. In that case, you, the higher-earning spouse, need to consider survivor's benefits when deciding the age to begin retirement benefits. A Social

Security *survivor's benefit* is the benefit payable to a surviving spouse after the other spouse passes away. The survivor's benefit is 100 percent of the benefit the deceased spouse was receiving. This section identifies some strategies you can use to ensure your spouse receives the maximum benefits after you're gone.

As the higher-earning spouse, you have to figure out how your decision regarding taking benefits affects your lower-earning spouse. Your goal should be to maximize the lifetime income of your spouse.

Strategy No. 1: Delay retirement benefits

You can increase the lifetime income of your lower-earning spouse if you delay retirement benefits, but only if you, the higher-earning spouse, die first. Delaying benefits is a form of free life insurance that provides extra income to the lower-earning spouse.

When both spouses are alive, the lower-earning spouse can receive the higher amount of his earned benefit or 50 percent of the higher-earning spouse's benefit at FRA. When the higher-earning spouse dies, the lower-earning spouse can't receive retirement benefits and a survivor's benefit. When someone is eligible for both types of benefits, he receives only the higher of the benefits. If the higher-earning spouse passes away, the surviving spouse either continues to receive his own earned benefit or receives 100 percent of the benefit that the higher-earning spouse was receiving before passing away.

The survivor's benefits rules should influence the age at which a higher-earning spouse decides to begin retirement benefits. For example, say the higher-earning spouse is eligible for $1,800 monthly at FRA, while the lower-earning spouse is eligible for an earned benefit of $700. If the lower-earning spouse chooses to take the spouse's benefit while the other spouse is still alive, he will receive $900 monthly, half of the higher-earning spouse's FRA benefit. The amount received by the higher-earning spouse (and the lower-earning spouse) will depend on the age her benefits began. Suppose she delayed benefits past FRA and receives $2,200 monthly. If the higher-earning spouse passes away first, the lower-earning spouse would then receive $2,200 monthly as a survivor's benefit. If the lower-earning spouse passes away first, the higher-earning spouse continues to receive only her earned benefit. Suppose instead the higher-earning spouse began benefits before FRA and was receiving $1,500 monthly. If the higher-earning spouse passes away first, the surviving spouse will receive $1,500 monthly.

Strategy No. 2: Begin benefits twice

The Social Security law allows married couples to use a strategy we coin "beginning your benefits twice," which can increase lifetime benefits. With this strategy, a spouse initially begins benefits, either his own earned benefit or a spousal benefit. After a few years, he switches to the other benefit. The strategy can maximize lifetime benefits, depending on which spouse earned more income and when each begins receiving earned retirement benefits.

For instance, consider the example in the earlier section "Choices for spousal benefits," where the lower-earning spouse began benefits based on his own earnings record because the higher-earning spouse hadn't yet begun receiving benefits. After the higher-earning spouse began benefits, the lower-earning spouse switched to spousal benefits based on the higher-earning spouse's earned benefit at FRA. In this case, the lower-earning spouse began benefits twice.

Similarly, a high-earning spouse can choose to receive spousal benefits based on the lower-earning spouse's benefits — even if that results in a lower monthly benefit —

and then later switch to a benefit based on her own earnings record.

Suppose, for example, the lower-earning spouse would be entitled to $1,000 monthly at FRA and the higher-earning spouse would receive $2,000 at FRA. They're both 62 years old. The lower-earning spouse begins benefits now, receiving $750 monthly. The higher-earning spouse wants to delay retirement benefits until age 70 to maximize lifetime benefits and also the survivor's benefit. To generate cash flow before then, at her FRA the higher-earning spouse applies for spousal benefits equal to one-half the lower-earning spouse's earned benefits at FRA, or $500. Then at age 70, the higher-earning spouse can apply for retirement benefits and begin receiving $2,000 monthly.

A higher-earning spouse who opts to receive spousal benefits based on her lower-earning spouse's benefits doesn't receive a reduction in her retirement benefits, because retirement benefits weren't applied for early. At the earlier age, only spousal benefits were applied for — and only at her FRA or later.

Identifying When You May Need to Receive Benefits

Social Security is an asset. It's a stream of income the government owes you. Like any asset, you need to manage Social Security to maximize lifetime income in a way that's consistent with your other goals and needs. When considering the time to begin drawing benefits, answer the questions in the following sections.

We address both a case of an individual deciding when to take benefits and also a case when a spouse is involved. The situation with a couple is a little more complicated. The couple can decide either to maximize lifetime benefits or to ensure that the lower-earning spouse receives the highest possible benefits if he survives the other spouse.

What are your cash flow needs?

If you need access to your benefits to pay expenses before you're eligible for full benefits, you probably have no choice but to begin receiving benefits early. If you've left the

_____

_____

_____

workforce, you may have limited sources of income. You may need to begin Social Security retirement benefits to pay living expenses as early as 62. Someone who still is in the workforce but on a part-time basis or at a reduced income may also need to begin benefits to meet expenses. If, however, you can continue to work and have investments or pensions that generate enough income to support your standard of living, you can afford to hold off on receiving benefits until your FRA or later.

Will waiting pay off?

When you don't have immediate need for retirement benefits before FRA, you may want to receive benefits based on the age that will generate the largest lifetime income. You can estimate this age by considering a simple trade-off: Begin retirement benefits early and you receive benefits for a longer period of time. Delay benefits and you receive a higher benefit. At some point, waiting to receive the large benefit is worthwhile.

So how do you know when you've reached this point? A simple way to decide is to calculate the rough *break-even point*. The break-even point is the year when the total lifetime benefits received from beginning benefits at a time other than

FRA equals the benefits that would be received from beginning benefits at FRA.

For example, say your benefit at FRA (age 66) is $1,400 per month. If you start benefits at 62, the benefit is reduced by 25 percent to $1,050, or $350 less per month. But, you receive the benefits for an extra 48 months. The total benefits received between 62 and FRA would be $50,400. Divide that by $350, and the result is 144. That's the number of months you would have to live beyond FRA to receive the same lifetime benefits as would be received by starting benefits at age 62. If you divide 144 by 12, you get 12 years. You would have to live to age 78 to reach the break-even point. If you live longer than the break-even point age of 78, you would come out ahead by $1,050 for each additional month lived.

Now, consider yourself in the same position but drawing benefits later. The benefit at age 70 would be $1,820 monthly, or 130 percent of the FRA benefit. Beginning benefits at 66 means receiving benefits for 48 extra months for a total of $67,200 of benefits received by age 70. Waiting until age 70 would result in an extra $420 per month. Divide the total benefits that would be received between ages 66 and 70 by the extra amount received by waiting until age 70. The result is 160. So it would take 160 months after age 70 for the lifetime payments received by beginning benefits at 70 to equal those received by beginning benefits at 66. If you divide 160 by 12, the result is 13.33 years. That means you would have to live another 13.33 years (until age 83 1/3) to reach the break-even point of receiving the same amount of lifetime benefits. If you live longer than 13.33 years, the lifetime benefits are higher by waiting.

After you calculate the break-even point, review the later section, "What's your life expectancy?" Doing so can give you a good idea of the probability you'll reach the break-even point should you choose to delay benefits.

In either of the preceding cases, you come out ahead by waiting to receive benefits if you live past the break-even point. If you pass away earlier, your lifetime benefits would be higher by taking benefits early.

What other income do you have?

If you have an investment portfolio or other income capable of paying living expenses, you have discretion over when to begin Social Security retirement benefits. By beginning benefits early, you have the option of leaving money invested instead of taking it out to pay expenses. Or you can invest the Social

Security benefits as received and continue spending the other sources of income.

Under either scenario you have an investment *side fund* that compounds until it's needed. You can assume an after-tax rate of return on this fund and estimate whether the fund would compound enough to justify taking lower benefits early instead of waiting for the higher benefits. If your side investment fund does well, the break-even point from waiting to begin benefits is pushed further into the future. (Refer to the preceding section "Will waiting pay off?" for more on break-even points.)

The problem with considering the results of an investing side fund is the uncertainty of investment returns. You can't assume a long-term average rate of return because you won't be investing for the long term. The projections of how well the side fund would perform would depend on your assumptions about investment returns and taxes. This area is where consulting with your accountant or financial planner can be helpful.

Do you want to continue to work?

Another factor to consider is any penalty for earned income received while receiving Social Security benefits. If you won't be working when receiving benefits, this isn't an issue. It also isn't an issue after FRA. But if you plan to work full or part time before FRA, you may earn so much that your benefits are reduced. In that case, it may not make sense to begin receiving benefits before FRA or until you stop working.

What are the potential income taxes on benefits?

You need to consider income taxes when deciding your beginning date for benefits. The general rule is that Social Security benefits are excluded from gross income when computing federal income taxes. But as income rises, a portion of the benefits may be included in your gross income. If your income is high enough to trigger taxes on the benefits after 62 but the income is likely to decline later, it may make sense to delay benefits until a smaller portion of them are taxed.

What's your life expectancy?

The key to choosing the best date to begin Social Security retirement benefits is by estimating how long you'll live.

_____

_____

_____

The benefit levels for different ages were calculated so a person who lives to life expectancy receives the same lifetime benefits regardless of when the benefits were begun. Life expectancy for an age group means half the people in the group will live longer and half will live shorter lives.

Of course, you don't know how long you will live, but here are a couple of factors to keep in mind when considering the issue:

- **Your personal health:** If you have a strong probability of living less than life expectancy (for example, you have a chronic disease that will shorten your life), receiving benefits as early as possible makes sense. Otherwise you may want to assume you'll be in the group that lives to life expectancy or longer.

- **Your family history:** If your family has a history of long life spans and you're in good health, you may consider delaying benefits to maximize lifetime payments.

Potential Income Taxes on Your Benefits

Originally Social Security retirement benefits were exempt from federal income taxes. However, in 1986, Congress made some benefits subject to income taxes. In 1993, more of the benefits paid to higher-income beneficiaries became subject to federal income taxes. The result is that the *marginal tax rate* (the tax rate on the last dollar of income earned) for some Social Security beneficiaries can be 70 percent or higher. Lower-income beneficiaries still receive all their benefits tax free, but higher-income beneficiaries can have up to 85 percent of benefits included in gross income.

As a result, you need to know when your Social Security retirement benefits may be subject to income taxes. This section explains how the taxes are calculated on your benefits and what you can do to lower yours.

How modified adjusted gross income works

The level of taxation of Social Security benefits depends on your *modified adjusted gross income*, or MAGI. MAGI is adjusted gross income (AGI) from your income tax return (before considering taxable Social Security benefits) plus one-half of your Social Security benefits and some types of exempt income (such as interest from tax-exempt bonds).

Your AGI is the amount left after subtracting from gross income deductions such as IRA contributions, self-employed health insurance premiums, and a few other expenses. Itemized expenses (such as mortgage interest and charitable contributions) and the standard deduction aren't subtracted to arrive at AGI. (*Tip:* You can find your AGI on the bottom of the first pages of Forms 1040 and 1040A and line 4 of Form 1040EZ.)

The main type of excluded income that's added back is *tax-exempt interest income.* This type of income is interest earned on debt issued by states and localities. Other types of exempt income to add back are interest from qualified U.S. savings bonds, employer-provided adoption benefits, foreign-earned income or foreign housing assistance, and income earned by bona fide residents of American Samoa or Puerto Rico.

So, if you're married and filing a joint return, Social Security benefits are taxed as follows:

> Up to 50 percent of benefits are included in gross income when MAGI is between $32,000 and $44,000.

Up to 85 percent of benefits are included in gross income when MAGI is more than $44,000.

If you're unmarried, Social Security benefits are taxed as follows:

Up to 50 percent of benefits are included in gross income when MAGI is between $25,000 and $34,000.

Up to 85 percent of benefits are included in gross income when MAGI is more than $34,000.

Benefits are included in gross income on a sliding scale. In other words, if you're married and filing jointly and your MAGI is $33,000, you don't include a full 50 percent of benefits in gross income. You include a portion of the benefits in income, but 50 percent of benefits isn't included in gross income until your MAGI equals $44,000.

IRS Publication 915, "Social Security and Equivalent Railroad Retirement Benefits," contains details about the taxation of benefits. It also has examples and worksheets to help you estimate the amount of benefits that are taxable. The publication is available free on the IRS website (www.irs.gov).

The SSA doesn't withhold income taxes on your benefits. You must make quarterly estimated tax payments to avoid incurring a penalty for underpayment of estimated taxes. You can find details of how much to pay and how to pay estimated taxes in Publication 505, "Tax Withholding and Estimated Tax," which also is available free on the IRS website. However, if you're taking IRA distributions or receiving a pension, you can request that the payor withhold income taxes. If enough is withheld, you'll avoid penalties for underpayment of income taxes without having to make quarterly estimated tax payments.

You also need to check with your state Department of Taxation or your tax advisor about how your state taxes Social Security benefits. Some states completely exempt Social Security benefits. Others piggyback on the federal system or tax the benefits at a different rate.

Reducing taxes on benefits

If your MAGI is in the range at which some of your benefits will be included in gross income, you may be able to take steps to reduce the taxes on your benefits.

_____

_____

_____

For a married couple, the amount of benefits included in gross income is determined by the joint MAGI. The tax on benefits isn't avoided or reduced by filing separate returns. In fact, for married couples filing separately, the benefits will be included in gross income when MAGI exceeds $0. On a joint return, the joint MAGI determines the level of benefits taxed. The taxes aren't computed separately on the benefits of each spouse. The joint income can cause benefits to be taxed even if only one spouse is receiving them.

If MAGI is significantly above the threshold at which benefits are taxed, planning strategies probably won't reduce the amount of benefits included in gross income. The changes would have to dramatically reduce MAGI to bring it close to or below the threshold.

Strategies to reduce taxes on your benefits

Almost all regular tax planning strategies that reduce MAGI can be used to reduce the amount of benefits included in gross income. These strategies include reducing gross income and increasing deductions for AGI. Remember that increasing itemized deductions, such as mortgage interest and charitable contributions, doesn't reduce MAGI. Here are strategies that are most likely to be valuable to you when reducing the taxes on your benefits:

- Minimize distributions from IRAs, pensions, and annuities. Don't take money from one of these vehicles unless you need it. Every dollar distributed to you is included in gross income and AGI. Consider tapping other sources, such as taxable investment accounts, first. If you have scheduled regular distributions from one of these vehicles, determine whether you can reduce the distributions. After age 70½, when required minimum distributions from IRAs and pensions are imposed, this strategy is more difficult. Before then, limiting distributions to those needed to pay expenses may reduce the amount of benefits that are taxed.

- Change investment strategies in taxable accounts to minimize gross income. Reduce trading in the account so capital gains are recognized less frequently. When gains are realized, sell investments in which you have losses to offset the gains. If the accounts hold mutual funds that frequently have high annual distributions, consider switching to funds with lower distributions.

_____

_____

_____

- Consider using taxable accounts to purchase deferred annuities. Income earned within an annuity is tax deferred; it won't increase MAGI as long as it remains in the annuity. In addition, annuities aren't subject to the required minimum distribution rules. For more information on annuities, see Chapter 7.

- Switch from taxable bonds to tax-exempt bonds. This move doesn't directly reduce the amount of Social Security benefits that are taxed. Tax-exempt interest is added back to AGI to reach MAGI. But the switch may indirectly reduce the tax on benefits because tax-exempt bonds usually pay lower interest rates than taxable bonds. When the tax-exempt interest is added back to AGI, it results in a lower MAGI than if the investments still were in higher-yielding taxable bonds.

- Shift income to family members other than your spouse. You don't want to shift assets that are needed to maintain your standard of living. But when assets and the income from them exceed your needs, consider transferring income-producing investments to other family members. This transferring should be done only as part of a comprehensive estate planning strategy with the reduction in taxes on Social Security benefits a side advantage.

Reducing your MAGI: Deduction strategies

The list in the preceding section includes ways you can reduce income and reduce MAGI. You also can take some deductions from gross income that can reduce MAGI. Even though itemized deductions (such as mortgage interest and charitable contributions) don't reduce taxes on Social Security benefits, the following deduction strategies may help:

- Sell capital assets that have paper losses. Many investors don't like to sell losing investments because the sale locks in the losses. A capital loss, however, can be used to your advantage. One advantage is that the loss reduces MAGI and therefore the amount of Social Security benefits included in gross income. Capital losses first are deducted against capital gains dollar for dollar. Each dollar of loss offsets a dollar of gains and reduces MAGI by a dollar. If the losses exceed the gains for the year, up to $3,000 of the losses are deducted against ordinary income. If you still have excess losses, they're carried forward to be used in future years in the same way.

- Examine your portfolio for investments with paper losses. Sell those investments and make the losses deductible. If you still like the long-term prospects for the investments, you can repurchase them. If they're securities (stocks, bonds, mutual funds), you have to wait more than 30 days to repurchase the same or substantially identical investments. If you don't wait, the loss deductions are deferred. If you don't want to wait to be back in the market, you can purchase investments that are similar but not substantially identical.

- Look for deductions for business losses. Eligible losses include those from partnerships, S corporations, and proprietorships. It may be possible to turn a hobby into a business that generates deductible losses. The losses are deductible if a profit is made in at least any three out of the last five consecutive years. The losses also can be deducted if the operation never earns a profit but is managed in a professional manner with the intention of making a profit.

9

Life Insurance

During your working years, especially your earlier working years, your future income earning ability is probably your most valuable asset. Consider that the typical person in his 20s and 30s has many years (decades, in fact) ahead of him to earn money to feed and clothe himself, make other expenditures, and save for the future. Unless you're independently wealthy, you should carry the proper type and amounts of insurance to protect yourself and your family if something occurs to you that would affect your ability to earn a living. In this chapter, we help you determine the life insurance you may need.

Insurance isn't free, of course. And, like other companies, insurance companies are in business to turn a profit. So you want to make sure you obtain proper insurance protection at a good price and buy only the coverage you need.

Assessing Your Need for Life Insurance

Needing insurance is kind of like needing a parachute: If you don't have it the first time you need it, chances are you won't need it again. Regarding your need for life insurance, of course, you don't get second chances. So, if you "need" life insurance, you should get it as soon as possible.

The following sections explain what life insurance can do for you. They also help you determine whether you need insurance, and if you do, how much you need.

The purpose of life insurance

The primary reason to consider buying life insurance is to provide financially for those who are dependent on your employment income. However, just because you have a job, earn employment income, and have dependents (children, a spouse, and so on) doesn't mean you need life insurance.

So how do you know whether you need life insurance coverage? Your current financial situation is an important factor in determining your need. If you haven't already assessed your retirement plan and tallied your assets and liabilities, be sure to read Chapter 2.

If you're still working, aren't financially independent, and need your current and future employment income to keep up your current lifestyle — and you're saving toward your financial goals — life insurance probably is a good choice. If you have others depending on your employment income, you generally should get term life insurance coverage (see the later section "What Type of Life Insurance to Buy").

On the other hand, you may find that even though you're still working, you've achieved financial independence. In other words, you've accumulated enough assets to be able to retire and no longer need to earn employment income.

Determining your life insurance need

We're not fans of general rules like getting ten times your annual income in coverage, especially for those approaching or already in their senior years. Each person's circumstances vary tremendously, so we don't tell you specifically how much life insurance to get. Instead, we show you the factors you need to look at to determine that amount. Consider the following:

- **Your assets:** Generally speaking, the more you have relative to your income and obligations, the less life insurance you need.

- **Your debts:** Of course, not all debts are created equal. Debts on real estate or small businesses tend to have lower interest rates, and the interest is tax deductible. But the more of this type of debt you have, the more life insurance you may need. On the other hand, consumer debt — such as credit card and auto loan debt — tends to be at higher interest rates, and the interest isn't tax deductible. But again, the more of this debt you have, the more life insurance you're likely to need.

- **Your health and the health of your family members:** If you have major medical problems or have a family member who's ill or who has special needs, you may need more coverage.

- **The number of children you need to put through college:** A four-year college education is a big expense. If you have kids to put through school — and they may attend costly schools — you could be talking some big bucks.

• **Whether you'll have elderly parents to assist:** Of course, this factor is difficult to predict, but you should have some sense of your parents' physical and financial health. If you don't, try to broach the topic in a sensitive fashion with them.

After completing your retirement planning (see Chapter 2), you should have the current financial information you need to begin your calculations for how much life insurance you need. Here's a quick and simple way to determine how much life insurance to consider buying:

1. **Determine your annual after-tax income (from working, not investments).**

   You can find this number on your tax return or W-2 form from the past year. (The reason you work with after-tax income is because life insurance death benefit payouts aren't taxed.)

2. **Determine the amount of money you need in order to replace your income for the appropriate number of years.**

   You can find this amount by simply using the information in Table 9-1.

3. **Consider your overall financial situation and whether you need to replace all of your income over the time period you chose in Step 2.**

   High-income earners who live well beneath their means may not want or need to replace all their income. If you're in this category and determine that you don't need to replace all your income, apply an appropriate percentage.

To Replace Your Income for This Many Years	Multiply Your Annual After-Tax Income by
5 years	5
10 years	9
15 years	12
20 years	15
25 years	17
30 years	19

Table 9-1: *Calculating Your Life Insurance Needs*

Assessing your current life coverage

 Before you rush out to buy life insurance, make sure you first assess how much coverage you may have through your employer and through Social Security.

The amount of coverage you have could reduce the amount you need to purchase independently. Employer-based life insurance coverage is an easier issue to deal with compared to Social Security survivor's benefits, so we address it first.

Employer-based life insurance

Some employers offer life insurance coverage. If it's free, by all means factor it into your calculations for how much additional coverage you may need. (Refer to the preceding section, "Determining your life insurance need," for more on calculating the coverage you need.)

For example, if your employer gives you $50,000 in life insurance without cost — and in Table 9-1 you calculated you should have $300,000 of coverage — simply subtract the $50,000 your employer provides to come up with $250,000 of life insurance you need to get on your own.

Keep in mind, however, if you leave the employer, you'll likely lose the provided insurance coverage. At that time, if your needs haven't changed, you'll need to replace the employer coverage.

_____

_____
_____

If you need to pay out of your own pocket for employer-based life insurance, it's generally not worth paying for. That's because group life plans tend to cost more than the least expensive individual life insurance plans.

You must be in good health to get life insurance on your own. If you have health problems, group coverage may be your best bet.

Social Security survivor's benefits

Social Security can provide survivor's benefits to your spouse and children. However, if your surviving spouse is working and earning even a modest amount of money, she's going to receive few to no survivor's benefits.

Before reaching Social Security's full retirement age, or FRA, your survivor's benefits get reduced by $1 for every $2 you earn above $16,920 (the limit for 2017). This income threshold is higher if you reach FRA during the year. (Check out Chapter 8 for more on FRA and Social Security benefits.)

If you or your spouse anticipate earning a low enough income to qualify for Social Security survivor's benefits, you may want to factor them into the amount of life insurance you calculate in Table 9-1. For example, suppose your annual after-tax income is $30,000 and Social Security provides a survivor's benefit of $12,000 annually. You calculate the annual amount of life insurance needed to replace like this:

$$\$30,000 - \$12,000 = \$18,000$$

Contact the Social Security Administration (SSA) to request Form 7004, which gives you an estimate of your Social Security benefits. To contact the SSA, call 800-772-1213 or visit www.ssa.gov.

What Type of Life Insurance to Buy

When looking to buy life insurance, you have two choices: term life insurance and cash-value insurance. The following sections outline these two and their differences and help you determine which may be better for your circumstance.

Term life insurance

Term life insurance is pure life insurance protection. It's 100 percent life insurance protection with nothing else, and, in our opinion, it's the way to go for the vast majority of people. Agents typically sell term life insurance as temporary coverage.

Remember that the cost of life insurance increases as you get older. You can purchase term life insurance so your premium steps up annually or after 5, 10, 15, or 20 years. The less frequently your premium adjusts, the higher the initial premium and its incremental increases will be.

The advantage of a premium that locks in for, say, 10 or 20 years is that you have the security of knowing how much you'll pay over that time period. You also don't need to go through medical evaluations as frequently to qualify for the lowest rate possible. Policies that adjust the premium every 5 to 10 years offer a happy medium between price and predictability.

The disadvantage of a term life insurance policy with a long-term rate lock is that you pay more in the early years than you do on a policy that adjusts more frequently. Also, your life insurance needs are likely to change over time. So you may throw money away when you dump a policy with a long-term premium guarantee before its rate is set to change.

Be sure that you get a policy that's guaranteed renewable. This feature assures that the policy can't be canceled because of poor health. Unless you expect that your life insurance needs will disappear when the policy is up for renewal, be sure to buy a life insurance policy with the guaranteed renewable feature.

Cash-value coverage

Cash-value coverage, also referred to as *whole life insurance,* combines life insurance protection with an investment account. For a given level of coverage, cash-value coverage costs substantially more than term coverage, and some of this extra money goes into a low-interest investment account for you. This coverage appeals to people who don't like to feel that they're wasting money on an insurance policy they hope to never use.

Agents usually sell cash-value life insurance as permanent protection. The reality is that people who buy term insurance generally hold it as long as they have people financially dependent on them (which usually isn't a permanent situation).

People who buy cash-value insurance are more likely to hold onto their coverage until they die.

Insurance agents often pitch cash-value life insurance over term life insurance. Cash-value life insurance costs much more and provides fatter profits for insurance companies and commissions to the agents who sell it. So don't be swayed to purchase this type unless you really need it.

Where to Buy Life Insurance

If you're going to purchase life insurance, you need to know where to go. You can look at the following two places:

- **Your local insurance agent's office:** Many local insur-ance agents sell life insurance, and you certainly can obtain quotes and a policy through them. As with any major purchase, it's a good idea to shop around. Don't get quotes from just one agent. Contact at least three. It costs you nothing to ask for a quote, and you'll prob-ably be surprised at the differences in premiums.

    As we discuss in the preceding section, many agents prefer to sell cash-value policies because of the fatter commissions on those policies. Don't be persuaded to purchase that type of policy if you don't think it's right for you.

- **An insurance agency quote service:** The best of these services provide proposals from the highest-rated, lowest-cost companies available. Like other agencies, the services receive a commission if you buy a policy from them, but you're under no obligation to do so.

  To get a quote, these services ask your date of birth, whether you smoke, some basic health questions, and how much coverage you want. Services that are worth considering include

- **AccuQuote:** www.accuquote.com; 800-442-9899

- **ReliaQuote:** www.reliaquote.com; 800-940-3002

- **SelectQuote:** www.selectquote.com; 800-963-8688

- **Term4Sale:** www.term4sale.com

10

Housing Decisions

Your housing needs change during your life, but they can really change in your retirement years. Life changes — such as ceasing work, kids growing up and moving out, divorce, death of a spouse, and so on — can have a dramatic impact on your housing wants and requirements and ability to afford housing.

In particular you face significant housing choices during your golden years. Most retirees grapple with moving, possibly downsizing, and moving into retirement communities that may offer health care. This chapter addresses these decisions you have to make and how the choices you make can potentially affect your finances. Additionally, we discuss reverse mortgages as a way to partly finance your retirement.

Analyzing Moving

Many folks move when they retire; they are motivated largely or in part by the attraction of reducing their expenses. Some lower their living costs, and some don't. Their happiness varies with their new locations as well. In this section, we discuss the appeal and realities of moving and the issues to weigh and contemplate.

The pros and cons of moving

Although many folks are content to and prefer to stay put when they retire, others wish to move. Among the primary motivations we've seen for retirees moving include the following:

- **Being closer to family and good friends:** Because jobs and careers take folks to locations that may not be their first or even second or third choices location-wise, it's no surprise that some retirees find themselves geographically isolated from their closest relatives and even best friends. Especially if you have adult children and possibly grandchildren living elsewhere, the pull to move closer to them can be strong.

_____

_____

_____

Clearly, moving closer to family and friends may have little or nothing to do with your finances, but that doesn't mean you should take the decision lightly. At a minimum, you should discuss your feelings and possible plans with the folks to whom you'd be moving near. Also, consider the possibility that someday these relatives may need or want to move somewhere else.

- **Living in a better climate:** With all the free time that retirement generally entails, climate escalates in importance for some people. Many older people prefer more temperate climates — that is fewer days of extreme heat or cold. Some folks with particular health conditions such as allergies or asthma find that moving to a temperate climate helps improve their symptoms and health.

- **Reducing their cost of living:** During their working years, many people live in more congested urban or near-urban areas with pricey housing and property taxes. If you have kids, you probably also are paying a premium to live in an area with better public schools. No longer constrained by where work is located or the need for access to good schools, you can consider moving to lower-cost areas.

- **Selecting housing that's user-friendly for the elderly:**
  As people age, their mobility and coordination inevitably decline, albeit at different rates for different people. So the housing you choose to live in during your younger years may no longer make sense. Steep driveways, stairways to the house and in the house, and other design issues may be decidedly unfriendly and potentially dangerous to your aging body.

Moving does have its downsides, however. And people often overlook them in the allure of believing the grass is greener elsewhere. Check out these drawbacks to moving:

- **Living costs may not decrease enough or at all.** The mistake too many folks make is that they assume their overall living costs will be lower after a move to an area that attracts them with, for example, lower-cost housing. You must and should examine all of your living expenses and how they may change with a proposed move.

- **You may introduce other negatives.** You may be successful in reducing your living costs with a move, but you also may find yourself in an area with other problems — more crime, traffic congestion, higher insurance costs on your home and car, and so on. Minimize your chances for disappointment by doing sufficient research before you make a decision to move.

- **Moving is costly.** Although you may be able to save money after your move is complete, be sure to make realistic estimates of your likely moving costs and how many years it will take to recoup them. The biggest expenses include real estate transaction costs and moving company costs.

To make an informed decision, do all of your homework and research concerning the topics discussed in this section. Don't focus on one reason to move. And don't make assumptions, such as your living costs will be lower because housing costs are less in a new community. Get the facts on how all of your living costs will change with a move. The best sources are people you know who already live there. You can consult official sources, such as chambers of commerce and realtors, but they may not be objective.

Options for where you can move

Traditional retirement living and housing choices are changing. New generations of retirees are looking for new living experiences, and developers are obliging, giving older Americans more choices for living arrangements than ever before. These new choices involve more than simply relocating outside the traditional retirement Sunbelt havens like Florida and Arizona. They also involve different types of housing and living arrangements and different types of activities in the communities.

One reason for the new senior living choices is that people are retiring earlier. At some adult communities, about one-third of residents are under age 65. Those under age 55 can make up 10 percent or more of the residents in some communities.

Another reason for the changes is that today's longer retirements have more stages than in the past, generally up to three stages. Each stage has a range of living choices. And, of course, not everyone goes through all of these stages or even any of them. The following sections identify some specific choices you have if you decide to move during retirement.

Stage No. 1: Downsizing

When folks downsize — that is, move to a smaller home — the goal is usually to maintain the same contacts and activities while shedding the labor and costs of maintaining a larger home. When you hit this stage, you've decided it's time to stop mowing the lawn, raking leaves, checking the gutters, and maintaining the mechanical systems. You also don't want to pay for rooms you aren't using.

You have several options for downsizing. You can move to a smaller house, townhouse, or condominium in a regular development. In this case, your neighbors will consist of those from all the age groups. Or you can move to a planned senior community (or age-restricted community) where people are similar in age, such as those we discuss in the next section.

Stage No. 2: Retirement communities

You may consider moving into a retirement community after you retire. If you're considering moving into a retirement community, make sure you look at the following factors:

- **The demographics of the community and how that appeals to you:** Some seniors prefer to be around people their own age; others prefer more diversity.

_____

_____

_____

If you're a young retiree, you may want to check the average age in a senior community because in some the average age is 75 or older. An adult community also may make you feel isolated from your family and friends, though you do have the opportunity to make new friends. A community that includes all ages may be noisier, less well kept, and keep later hours. You may want to visit at different times of the day and week to get a good flavor of the lifestyle.

- **The types of activities offered on-site and in the surrounding community:** Each type of community will have its own activities, plus the activities in the surrounding community. A development built for seniors may provide services that are helpful to seniors, such as laundry, housecleaning, and on-grounds restaurants. Many newer senior communities also have amenities such as spas, golf courses, and health clubs. They can be more like resorts or country clubs than traditional adult communities or regular developments. Also, be sure to consider how your current activities would be affected.

Stage No. 3: Housing that's near family and has healthcare

The third stage of retirement often involves moving near friends and family, especially grandchildren, and moving into traditional senior housing with some healthcare facilities on premises. This stage has four basic choices when it comes to housing:

- **Independent living:** This essentially entails living in an apartment or condo complex for seniors. As part of your monthly rental you get some basic services, such as housekeeping, transportation, activities, and some meals.

- **Assisted living:** This type of housing offers additional services and is for someone who needs help with two or more of the basic activities of daily living (bathing, dressing, walking, and so on). You may be able to avoid or delay this option by having in-home care at your existing residence.

- **Nursing home:** This option is for someone who needs daily medical care help.

- **Continuing care retirement community (CCRC):** This option bundles all the preceding living arrangements into one. You can start in independent living or assisted living, and as your needs change, you're guaranteed a place in the other types of care. You only have to move to another location in the same community instead of having to look for a different facility and moving there. CCRCs are being built all over the country.

There's no one right answer in terms of housing. Each person's situation and preferences are unique, so we advise that you explore your options and select the choice that feels right for your situation. Your doctor or other medical professional may direct you to one of the options. You also may find objective advice from your local Area Office on Aging.

Reverse Mortgages

If you own the same home during most of the decades of your adult life, you probably will have some decent equity accumulated in it. You may wish to tap that equity to supplement your retirement income. For example, you can sell your home, buy a smaller, less costly property, and use the profit you make to finance your retirement.

Another way to tap into your equity is through a *reverse mortage*, which enables you through a loan to receive tax-free income on your home's equity while still living in the home.

The following sections outline the specifics of reverse mortgages, including how they work and how to determine whether one is right for you.

Defining terms and costs

With a reverse mortgage, the lender pays you (via lump sum, monthly payments, or a credit line), and the accumulated loan balance and interest is paid off when your home is sold or you pass away. The typical borrower is a widow who is 70+ years old and running out of money, wants to stay in her home, and needs money for basic living expenses or for important home-maintenance projects such as replacing a leaky roof.

Here are the basic standards of eligibility:

- You, the homeowner, must be at least 62 years of age.

- You must use the home as your principal residence.

- Any outstanding debt against the home must be paid in full.

Retirees who have taken a reverse mortgage generally say it has been a good experience. They often cite that the extra income allowed them to keep up a home's maintenance, pay medical and other expenses, avoid having to scrimp so much on things like eating out occasionally, and gain peace of mind not having to make house payments.

Reverse mortgages aren't free of drawbacks. Keep the following in mind:

- **The effective interest rate can vary greatly.** With their high upfront costs, the effective interest rate (which factors in all the fees and interest you pay relative to the number of years you keep the loan) on most reverse mortgages easily jumps into the double-digit realm if you only stay a few years into the loan.

- **They can be complicated to understand and compare.** Your effective interest rate varies greatly depending on how long you're in the home and using the loan, the timing and size of payments you receive, and your home's value over time.

On the flip side, some aspects to qualifying for and having a reverse mortgage are easier than with a traditional mortgage. Consider the following:

_____

_____

_____

- **You don't need to have any income.** Income isn't important because you're not making any payments. The loan balance is accumulating against the value of your home, and it gets paid when the home is sold.

- **You don't need good credit.** You're not borrowing money, so your credit score doesn't matter.

- **You can't lose your home for failing to make payments because there are none.** Reverse mortgages are *non-recourse loans,* which means that the lender can't take your home if you default on the loan.

Determining whether a reverse mortgage is right for you

To consider whether a reverse mortgage may make sense for you, consider the following:

- **Start with nonfinancial considerations.** Do you want to keep your current home and neighborhood? What's your comfort level with the size of your home and the associated upkeep? Consider whether you want to stay in your home for the foreseeable future or would rather tap into your home's equity by moving and downsizing to a smaller home or by simply renting.

_____

_____

_____

- **Discuss your explorations and concerns with your family.** Make sure everyone is aware of the range of options. Discussion may lead you to a better solution.

- **Understand what a reverse mortgage can do for you compared to a home equity loan.** Part of the appeal of a reverse mortgage is the lack of attractive alternatives if you'd like to stay in your home. For example, with a home equity loan, the big challenges are qualifying for a loan when you have limited income and making the required payments when you do get a loan. Home equity loans are *recourse loans*, which means if you're unable to keep up with payments later in retirement, the lender can foreclose.

If you're seriously considering a reverse mortgage, you may have more questions about the specifics that we don't cover in this chapter. If so, visit the AARP website at www.aarp.org/revmort for lots of helpful information.

_____

_____

_____

About the Authors

Eric Tyson is an internationally acclaimed and best-selling personal finance author, syndicated columnist, and speaker. He has worked with and taught people from all financial situations, so he knows the financial concerns and questions of real folks just like you. Despite being handicapped by an MBA from the Stanford Graduate School of Business and a BS in economics and biology from Yale University, Eric remains a master of "keeping it simple." After toiling away for a number of years as a management consultant to Fortune 500 financial-service firms, Eric took his inside knowledge of the banking, investment, and insurance industries and committed himself to making personal financial management accessible to all. Eric's website is www.erictyson.com.

Bob Carlson is editor of the monthly newsletter, *Retirement Watch,* and a weekly free e-newsletter, *Retirement Watch Weekly.* Bob also is chairman of the board of trustees of the Fairfax County Employees' Retirement System, which has over $2.8 billion in assets. He has served on the board since 1992. He was a member of the Board of Trustees of the Virginia Retirement System, which oversaw $42 billion in assets, from 2001 to 2005. Bob received his JD and an MS (accounting) from the University of Virginia, received his BS (financial management) from Clemson University, and passed the CPA exam. He also is an instrument-rated private pilot.